Praise for Bleed a Creed

"*Bleed a Creed* is the essential playbook for building a purposeful brand and organization. You will be inspired to build your own business with a unique point of view and armed with lessons to make it happen."
  —Eric Ryan, co-founder, method and OLLY

"A veteran practitioner of purpose, Matt has created a practical roadmap to seizing the opportunities that purpose unleashes. This book is a powerful resource for anyone who's on the purpose journey — whether starting out or climbing its peaks."
  —Roy Spence, co-founder & chairman, GSD&M /
  co-founder & CEO, The Purpose Institute

"Matt Carcieri knows the key insight to successful branding practice: consumers don't just buy brands, they live lives; and into those lives, successful brands with purpose come. Read this rich workbook and benefit from Matt's wisdom, experience and frameworks to help your brand lead a purpose-driven life."
  —Susan Fournier, Allen Questrom Professor and Dean,
  Boston University Questrom School of Business

"When the alarm rings at 5:30 and your first thought is market share or market cap, just go back to sleep. You're missing the point. And the rewarding path. And the rich possibilities . . . as Matt Carcieri reveals."
  —Bob Garfield, co-host of *On the Media* and coauthor of *Can't Buy Me Like*

"Matt has catalyzed a movement across our company that is step-changing engagement and innovation. In this book, he shares the tools of his trade, providing a concrete roadmap to unleashing the full power of purpose."
  —Jeff Boutelle, CEO, Pharmavite

"Matt completely redefined my company based on these principles, and it allowed us to shoot from last place in our category to second. *Bleed a Creed* shows you the path to get there."
  —Greg Stuart, Global CEO, Mobile Marketing Association

"Matt has helped us immensely on our Purpose journey to drive competitive advantage by inspiring our people. I highly recommend him and this book as your guide to help you carve your own path."
  —Jason Anderson, Senior Vice President Marketing, Cadillac Fairview

Bleed a Creed

How to Create and Activate
a Powerful Brand Purpose

Matt Carcieri

Foreword by Jim Stengel

Paramount Market Publishing, Inc.

Paramount Market Publishing, Inc.
274 North Goodman Street, STE D-214
Rochester, NY 14607
www.paramountbooks.com
607-275-8100

Publisher: James Madden
Editorial Director: Doris Walsh

Cataloging in Publication Data available
ISBN-13: 978-1-941688-62-5 *hardcover*
eISBN-13: 978-1-941688-63-2

For my mom and dad —

for teaching me the wisdom of values

and the beauty of devotion

Whatever is hard to be traversed,
whatever is hard to be acquired,
whatever is hard to be visited,
whatever is hard to be performed,
all this may be accomplished by true devotion;
for the difficulty of devotion is the greatest of all.

— from the ancient Hindu "Laws of Manu"

Contents

Foreword

In late 2018, the largest U.S. marketing trade group, the Association of National Advertisers (ANA), asked its members to vote on the marketing word of the year. "Brand purpose," albeit two words, was the hands-down winner. I immediately tweeted, "How about the 'marketing word' of the decade? Or 21st century?"

The groundswell of businesses reorienting their strategy and culture on a higher-order purpose is arguably unprecedented as a movement across industry at large. And unlike Henry Ford's pioneering work on assembly lines in the early 1900s, or Edward Deming's innovative work on total-quality management in the mid-twentieth century, or Brené Brown's recent work on vulnerability and courage, there is no one person or entity that defines the movement.

No one could have predicted at the start of this century that the largest asset manager in the world, BlackRock, would tell the CEOs of the world's largest companies that they would need to serve a social purpose while growing profits, or risk losing support from BlackRock. No one could have predicted that one of the most watched videos this century was from Simon Sinek, at the time an unknown author, who urged leaders to "Start with Why." And, in any given week, books about purpose in business are on the best-sellers list.

So what can Matt Carcieri possibly add to this large and still-growing purpose movement with his many-years-in-the-making *Bleed a Creed*?

A lot. Here's why you should read on: Matt is one of the few people in the world who has committed his life to helping senior leaders from financial services to pharmaceuticals to snacks *discover* and *activate* their purpose – or better yet, their creed – for the past twenty years. His knowledge is real and tested. His approach works.

But beyond his twenty years as a practitioner of purpose, what is special about Matt is that he is a born teacher. The following pages glow with his passion for growing businesses through purpose; but as importantly, Matt has synthesized and codified his learning into an inspiring, story-rich workbook for any leader . . . wherever he or she is on the purpose journey.

You may be new to Matt. I'm not. I spotted Matt when I was the Global Marketing Officer of P&G. He was a rising star who could not stop talking about the potential of P&G's brands pivoting on purpose. I was on a mission to inspire and invigorate P&G's marketing people to make a larger impact on consumers' lives through our brands, which I was convinced would restart growth (and it did). Matt became one of my inner circle and one of P&G's catalysts to rethink how P&G builds brands.

Matt and I both left P&G in the late 2000s, and we teamed up again as part of my think tank/consulting group. Since P&G, we have worked with more than one hundred businesses who want to accelerate growth by following the principles in this book.

So read on. This has been a labor of love for Matt. You will feel that. And you will also feel compelled to act. The good news is that *Bleed a Creed* will show you the way.

—JIM STENGEL
Former Global Marketing Officer, P&G
Founder & CEO, The Jim Stengel Group
Senior Fellow, Kellogg/Northwestern

Preface

I'll never forget the anticipation I felt as my wife and I drove through the mountains of West Virginia into the open expanse of Ohio. I had just finished business school, and I was en route to a new career at Procter & Gamble, chasing after my interest in brand building. I was eager to learn from the wizards there and find out what makes great brands tick. As the highway unfolded before us, it felt a little like the yellow brick road to the Emerald City.

For the next decade, I managed iconic brands like Pringles, Folgers, and Pantene. Like every good P&Ger, I mastered the company's best practices but, at the same time, was dissatisfied with the status quo. Along the way, I developed the conviction that P&G needed to push its brand building into new territory: the higher ground of brand purpose. The inspiration was everywhere. Internally, Pampers had found breakout success with a high-order "reason why." Looking outside our walls, I marveled at Apple, Dove, Zappos, Whole Foods, Starbucks, Nike, and Method.

With a new sense of personal purpose, I breached the tower where the actual wizards live — a group of corporate content experts, masters in the realm of brand building. I took on a role that gave me responsibility for P&G's best practices in brand strategy. Now, not only was I immersed in P&G's brand-building playbook, I was one of its authors.

In that role, I jumped on the front end of this decade's "purpose boom." With air cover from then-CMO Jim Stengel, I delved deeply into the art and science of purposology and spearheaded "why" work on over twenty P&G brands, including most of the company's billion-dollar icons. On several brands — like Secret and even Charmin — we saw some exciting outcomes. But with every success, we also experienced a couple of duds: brands where the impact and results were uninspired. In that brew, I learned a lot about the alchemy of purposeful success.

I left P&G several years ago to enter consulting, and I've now had the opportunity to work with over one hundred brands and companies on purpose. Along the way, I've continued to learn about the mechanisms of purpose.

Ever since my days at P&G, I've been motivated to develop best practices in order to raise people's capability and the performance of their businesses. That's the drive that led me to write this book. In a happy convergence, writing about purpose fulfills my purpose.

START-UP
The Purpose Challenge

The difficulty of devotion is the greatest of all.
— from the ancient Hindu "Laws of Manu"

The New Soul of Business

If you're like most business leaders today, you believe in the power of purpose. That makes you part of one of the biggest movements in the history of business. Like a glacier reshaping the contours of commerce, purpose is fundamentally changing the discipline of management, the experience of employees, the fruits of capitalism, and the future of the world.

Although "purpose" as a term is getting a lot more attention these days, the concept and practice have been around for centuries. For as long as there's been industry, enlightened leaders have framed their businesses around idealistic aims. Upon the founding of Johnson & Johnson in 1886, Robert Wood Johnson declared that his surgical-dressings start-up existed to "alleviate pain and disease." Walt Disney created his company with the aim to "bring happiness to millions." And William Hesketh Lever, the founder of Lever Brothers, set out to "make cleanliness commonplace."

While purpose isn't new, its role and location in the ecosystem of business has become much more central. That change started happening in the 1990s and accelerated dramatically this decade. A number of forces brought the business world to an inflection point: the maturation of consumerism, the narrowing of functional product differences, a digitally empowered consumer base, a generational quest for meaning, the sustainability imperative, etc. As a result, the public discourse about purpose increased fivefold over the span of a decade.[1]

Another big reason for the prevalence of purpose is the growing body of proof that it correlates to better business results. Over the last 25 years, multiple studies have affirmed a link between strong purpose and strong performance:

- In their 1994 classic *Built to Last*, authors Jim Collins and Jerry Porras identified a set of breakout companies that, as a central element of their success, had a "sense of purpose beyond just making money." Collectively, they outperformed comparison companies six-to-one.[2]

- In 2007, the Wharton-published book *Firms of Endearment* examined 28 companies operating with purpose. Over a ten-year period, the set beat the S&P by an eight-to-one margin.[3]

- In 2011, my colleague Jim Stengel ran a study with Millward-Brown Optimor, which he featured in his book *Grow*. Using Millward-Brown's Brand Z database of fifty thousand brands, the study looked at financial and consumer results over a ten-year timeframe and found that the majority of the leading companies were purpose-driven and grew three times faster than competition.[4]

- An "Insights 2020" study sponsored by several organizations, including the Advertising Research Foundation, found that 80 percent of companies that over-perform on revenue growth link everything they do to purpose.[5]

- Academic research published in 2016 — using data from the Great Places to Work Institute — found that firms "exhibiting both high purpose and clarity" had systematically higher stock market performance.[6]

- In an analysis of its 2017 "Best Global Brands," Interbrand found that brands with a purpose outperformed the stock market by 120 percent.[7]

So you're right: purpose is indeed powerful. When properly defined and fully activated, it can transform a business and brand. Purpose can't cover up for gaps in operational basics (Chipotle is a cautionary tale), but when it takes root amidst strong fundamentals, it can unleash greater vitality — both inside and in market.

Purpose Defined

So what exactly is a "purpose?" I define it as the business's inspirational 'reason for being' beyond making money. It's the definitive difference the organization seeks to make in the world. It represents the high-order motivation that you share with your consumers.

Your business's purpose is its inspirational 'reason for being' beyond making money.

Purpose can exist at either the enterprise or brand level. In some cases, like Apple and Twitter, the corporate enterprise and the brand are one and the same. But in others, like Estée-Lauder and Unilever, the corporate enterprise houses a number of individual brands. In those multi-brand companies, purpose exists at two levels: one for the corporate parent and a unique purpose for each of the individual product or service brands. For example, the purpose of Diageo, the maker of spirits like

Captain Morgan, is to "celebrate life, every day, everywhere." The purpose of Captain Morgan is to "inspire people with the power of fun." Within a corporate-brand "purpose architecture," the alignment of purposes should work top-down like a light cast through a prism. The purposes of the individual brands are "refractions" of the corporate value system — related but distinct.

Related but Different Concepts

Although the terms are often used interchangeably, a purpose is different than a mission or vision. A company or brand purpose is the expression of its "why": why the business exists. A mission articulates "what": what value proposition the brand provides in support of its purpose. This is sometimes referred to as the brand's "promise." A vision lays out "where": where the business aims to be in the future. As an illustration, below are the different elements for Southwest Airlines and IKEA:

Southwest Airlines	
Purpose	To connect people to what's important in their lives
Mission	By providing friendly, reliable and low-cost air travel
Vision	To become the world's most loved, most flown and most profitable airline
IKEA	
Purpose	To create a better everyday life for the many people
Mission and Vision	To offer a wide range of well-designed, functional home furnishing products and services at prices so low that as many people as possible will be able to afford them

Purpose is often muddled with another hot topic in business: corporate social responsibility. Some people call this "social purpose," which is an unhelpful term in that it only exacerbates the confusion. While purpose is about high-order direction setting, CSR is more operational in nature. It refers to practices that have a direct and specific impact: either addressing a societal ill or minimizing a negative impact generated in the conduct of the business.

Under the banner of CSR, there are three, broad sub-disciplines: philanthropy, cause marketing and sustainability. Philanthropy and cause marketing apply business resources toward the improvement of a specific societal condition. Sustainability, meanwhile, focuses on minimizing the negative effects of business operations. This may involve employee welfare and other issues but most commonly refers to the "greening" of the business. All of these programmatic priorities – like all business activities – fall under the broad umbrella of the brand or company purpose. They are inspired by and informed by the business's high-order "reason why."

As an example, consider LEGO, which was ranked by the Reputation Institute as the top CSR company in 2017.[8] LEGO's purpose is to "inspire and develop the builders of tomorrow." That 'reason for being' directs all aspects of the company's endeavors – from its product offerings to its advertising. One of those endeavors is its CSR, which includes two major initiatives. The first is "Build the Change," a series of local events around the world that engage children in developing ideas for a brighter future. The second is its Sustainable Materials Center. Backed by an investment of $150 million, the center aims to find non-petrochemical sources for its building materials by 2030.[9]

The Five Opportunities of Purpose

Purpose is a transformational force for business because it offers the potential for breakthroughs in five areas: employee engagement, innovation generation, societal contribution, brand relevance, and consumer attention. Notably, these five outcomes are not automatic by-products; but purpose opens the door to their pursuit. As such, I call them "the five opportunities of purpose." Because purpose is sometimes thought of as a brand's "North Star," we can use that metaphor as a model — showing the five opportunities as offshoots from a core.

Employee Engagement

The first and most significant opportunity of purpose is employee engagement. By providing a source of collective inspiration, purpose motivates your workforce and keeps everyone rowing in the same direction. It gives meaning to work and inspires excellence and creativity. According to a 2014 survey by Deloitte, 73 percent of employees who report working for a purpose-driven company say they're engaged, compared with just 23 percent of those who don't.[10] And research by PricewaterhouseCoopers found that Millennials are five times more likely to stay with a company when they have a strong connection to its purpose.[11]

Innovation Generation

Purpose fuels perpetual value creation. The call to "serve" people and the world unleashes a never-ending cycle of innovation. According to a 2014 survey by Deloitte, organizations with a high-order purpose are two times more likely to invest in new technologies.[12] Purpose also inspires growth across platforms and helps produce a more meaning-filled experience for customers. All that leads to a more valuable business. In a related piece of research, global banking giant HSBC found that Millennial entrepreneurs are achieving greater success than older generations because they are motivated by purpose over profit.[13]

Societal Contribution

Purpose opens the aperture to a broader group of stakeholders and inspires contributions that directly benefit society. Not only is the world advantaged by these acts; but the enterprise realizes gains as well — in the form of goodwill. In today's marketplace, that goodwill is vital to the success of your business. Fifty-one percent of job candidates won't work for your company if it doesn't demonstrate strong social and environmental commitments.[14] And 85 percent of consumers say they prefer brands that behave responsibly.[15]

Brand Relevance

Purpose offers the opportunity to make your brand more relevant and resonant among your target consumers. That's because the persuasive power of passion and shared values lures in new customers and fosters loyalty among values cohorts. According to Kantar Consulting, nearly two-thirds of Millennials and Gen Z express a preference for brands that have a point of view and stand for something. That purposeful resonance fuels brand strength. Confirming those findings, research powerhouse Millward-Brown reports, "Analysis of key brands in the Top 100 over the past decade shows that brands with a stronger purpose – that is, brands that are perceived to make consumers' lives better and seem to put purpose before profit – also create greater brand equity."[16]

Consumer Attention

Finally, purpose offers the potential for greater levels of consumer attention – through the power of cultural movements. To get the meaningful attention that your brand needs for growth, it has to grab a share of the popular culture. It has to be picked up by social media and carried aloft. Championing a cause, confronting an issue, asserting a point of view – these are the most potent fuel sources for igniting consumers' interest in your brand. According to research by communications agency Edelman, consumers are more likely to advocate for a brand after hearing about its stand (32 percent) than its product features (26 percent).[17]

Troubles in Purpose Paradise

With all the benefits that purpose promises — and all the buzz surrounding the topic — it's likely that you're already working to adopt the purpose agenda on your business. But it's also likely that you're not enjoying all of its glories. In fact, a survey by EY found that only a minority of executives feel that their organizations are successfully operating in a purpose-driven way.[18] The purpose hasn't grabbed employees' hearts and minds. It doesn't act as a force of daily governance. And while 76 percent of marketing leaders say their organization has a defined purpose, only one in ten says the organization has a meaningful plan to activate it.[19]

On the marketing effectiveness front, you may be feeling less than stellar as well. Yours may be one of the many organizations that has either failed to spark breakthrough or stumbled in the activation of purpose. It's tricky business, and reliably, every Super Bowl features some high-profile fumbles. In 2017, 84 Lumber drew scorn for its baffling, seemingly co-opted immigration drama. In 2018, viewers scratched their heads when the renegade T-Mobile brand gave soft support for the equality movement, and they got downright indignant when Dodge wrapped itself in a Martin Luther King Jr. sermon to hawk its Ram trucks. Outside of the Super Bowl, the poster child for "purpose abuse" is Pepsi's infamous film featuring Kendall Jenner, in which she tries to inject some sugar and fizz into the tension of a protest march. Most viewers saw it as being blatantly exploitative — a domain where the brand had no right to play. In 2019, Gillette faced backlash as well, after taking a stand against toxic masculinity. Because of the un-heroic tone of the ad, many male viewers felt scolded by their classic hero brand.

As with every major progression in culture, there's now a counter-movement against "goodwashing." *Saturday Night Live* gave it a good slap in a skit about a pitch meeting for a new Cheetos ad. After dismissing an ad idea about family fun, the clients get wildly enthused about Alec Baldwin's melodramatic depiction of a purpose-driven spot. "We open on a Mexican person wearing a sombrero," the ad exec says over a tenderly concerned music track. "He takes it off. Underneath is a Muslim woman." Under her hijab is a Jewish person, and underneath his yarmulke is a Cheeto. "We are one" is the ad's slogan.[20]

Common Problem Spots

So what's the problem? Why aren't more brands more success-ful in embedding and activating purpose? Why does the linkage between a brand and its purposeful marketing sometimes feel so phony and frayed?

Having worked with over one hundred companies and brands on purpose, I see some common problem spots, and I put them all under the headline of devotion. The first is the purpose itself. Often it doesn't represent a heartfelt devotion that's authentic to the DNA of the enterprise. The purpose is a platitude. There's no burning conviction.

In many cases, the issue starts at the very beginning: with a flawed conception of purpose. For most businesspeople today, purpose is seen as a service agenda — putting the brand in ser-vice to people, the world and its socio-environmental priorities. In this frame, purpose equates to societal benefit. All of that is good and noble and right; but it's not the full picture. In its most effective form, purpose is not only a service agenda; it's also a *values* agenda. Underlying the purpose — as fuel for the purpose — there's a definitive point of view, a clear "enemy," and a vision for how the world should be. The organization has a unique "creed" that unlocks the full promise of purpose. Often, that authentic organizational devotion is missing, and "green marketing" grows over top.

Another common issue is a lack of commitment to the ongoing work of turning the opportunities of purpose into realities. Too often, leadership walks out of a purpose definition session inspired by the outcome but doesn't follow through on activation and the sustained effort it requires. More often than not, the organization doesn't display the courage and put in the sweat that's required to:

- Create an internal culture in which employees are aligned with – and engaged in – the brand's purpose.
- Develop offerings that are uniquely purposeful and stretch the brand into new platforms.
- Embed social contribution into the core operations of the business.
- Build a brand identity that telegraphs the organization's driving intent.
- Make waves in the popular culture, spurring positive change and moving the world closer to the brand's desired end state.

Effective activation requires leaders to put their time, talent and treasure where their purposeful tenets are. Otherwise, the purpose remains a superficial and ineffective overlay. It ends up sitting above the enterprise but doesn't penetrate the mechanics of the business.

Where This Book Comes In

In the chapters that follow, I'll try to help you overcome the purpose challenge: the challenge of finding a true devotion and devoting your organization to the work of pursuing all five opportunities. In the course of each chapter, I'll build the case for the priority and then present specific levers for taking action. The priorities for activation will flow from the inside out: from embedding to operationalizing to advocating.

In Chapter 1 (Have a Point of View), I'll make the case that great purpose starts with a definitive "creed," which includes convictions and values. I'll give you a compass tool to help you navigate the values landscape and invite you to explore your brand's unique angle on the world. In Chapter 2 (Craft Your Creed), I'll lay out the elements of a brand creed and walk you through the process of discovering and articulating your brand's unique point of view and purpose.

Chapter 3 (Engage Your Organization) addresses the first of the five opportunities. It makes the case for building a culture of purpose and presents a model with nine specific levers for bringing your creed to life inside. Of all the activation priorities (and chapters), it is the biggest.

In Chapter 4 (Develop Offerings with Intent), I'll offer guidance on translating your purpose into your product experience and generating purposeful innovation. Chapter 5 (Display Social Commitment) makes the case for wiring social contribution into your core operations and outlines four approaches for doing so. Chapter 6 (Brand with Values) describes how a creed fosters increased brand relevance and outlines two levers for communicating your creed externally. Finally, Chapter 7 (Be a Protagonist) will show you how to apply your creed to grow your share of popular culture and gain consumer attention.

I've derived the guidance in this book from three sources: thousands of hours of independent research, my collaborations with purpose luminaries like Jim Stengel, Roy Spence, and Joey Reiman, and my firsthand experience engaging with hundreds of purpose-inspired brands and companies. In addition, several of the insights come from original research conducted by my colleague Dr. Chris Allen, Professor Emeritus at the University of Cincinnati. In 2013–2014, Chris did 41 interviews at eight firms that we deemed to have strong, purpose-fueled cultures. They included Method, Innocent Drinks, Discovery Communications, and Motorola Solutions. He and I published the findings of that research in a compendium entitled *Brand Touchpoints,* edited by Aparna Sundar (Nova Science Publishing, 2018).

By the conclusion of this book, I hope you'll overcome the all-too-prevalent purpose challenge. I hope you'll have a truly compelling brand purpose – one that arises from a distinctive creed – and I hope the five opportunities of purpose will become your realities. Ultimately, I hope that, as a byproduct of this book, more leaders and organizations will "bleed a creed," and as a result, more companies, employees, and consumers will benefit from the fruits of purpose.

CHAPTER 1
Have a Point of View

Strong convictions precede great actions.
—*James Freeman Clarke*

Leading with Conviction

The last of the seven Lincoln-Douglas debates took place in Alton, Illinois on October 15, 1858. Among the five thousand people in attendance, a large number had traveled from the neighboring slave state of Missouri, paying one dollar for a round-trip steamboat ride across the Mississippi. As was typical of these popular debates, the crowd was feisty.

Undaunted, Senate candidate Abraham Lincoln made his case against slavery. He emphatically condemned the "tyrannical principle" of one race or class bestriding another. To him, it was patently un-American. Had it not been immoral for the King of England to live off the fruits of the colonists' labors? With firm conviction, he declared that slavery mirrored the very injustice that America was born to resist: the "divine right of kings."[1]

The future mayor of Alton, Henry McPike, was seated on the dais that day, and years later, he remembered how profoundly Lincoln had touched his soul. What affected him most was the way the candidate spoke. In his remarks about the sinfulness of slavery, Lincoln had exhibited "the earnestness of a heart convinced." "So long as I live I will never lose the impression he made upon me," McPike said.[2]

Like all great leaders, Lincoln's impact arose from a heartfelt conviction. From years of lovingly studying the nation's founding documents — and influenced by the events of his time — he came to a point of view that would motivate his political life and propel his leadership through America's bloodiest war. In the face of crushing turmoil and counterforces, he held to his core convictions and values, resolving, "I must keep some standard of principle fixed within myself."[3]

To many, strength of conviction is the very essence of leadership. The condition of feeling moved is the precursor to moving and motivating others. It's the antecedent to action. Steve Jobs had this to say on the subject: "You have to be burning with an idea, or a problem, or a wrong that you want to right. If you're not passionate enough from the start, you'll never stick it out."[4]

Not only do great leaders exhibit impassioned points of view, so do great brands and businesses:

- Southwest grew to its loved and large status on the conviction "that flight should not be limited to the well-to-do, but that it should be an opportunity for all: that people should have the freedom to fly."

- Brothers John and Bert Jacobs created a $100 million t-shirt and merchandise business — without any advertising — on the heartfelt contention that "Life is Good."[5]

- Fox News has built a loyal following on its conviction that the mainstream media (or "MSM" as it terms it) has a liberal bias.

- Driven by Danny Thomas' conviction that "no child should die in the dawn of life," St. Jude Children's Research

Hospital has helped improve the survival rate of child-hood cancer from 20 percent to 80 percent.[6]

· Nike started its incredible run to $120 billion in market cap with the conviction that "there is no finish line."[7] CEO Mark Parker says:

> We believe in potential, not limits. The 4-minute mile was safe, until Roger Bannister. Lou Gehrig's 2,130 straight games was safe, until Cal Ripken. No one would ever clear 29 feet in the long jump, until Bob Beamon. Nobody would ever beat Bob Beamon, until Michael Powell. That's how it is with NIKE. We believe.[8]

These are just a few of the businesses that have a fervent point of view that propels their success. All of them are driven by purpose, but compared to many other "purpose-driven" organizations, these companies have higher-octane fuel in the purpose tank. Their purposes derive from bedrock convictions about life and the world. In other words, their purpose isn't a platitude; it's a passion. Their sense of purpose is belief-inspired – the activation of a heartfelt devotion. That is to say, there are life-level convictions that *precede* the purpose.

The most successful brands have life-level convictions that *precede* their purpose.

More than purpose, conviction-fueled entities have inten-tion. While purpose is commonly defined as a desired end or aim, intention means "determining mentally upon some action or result." In its Latin root, it means "to turn one's attention to; to be in quest of something; to be zealous." Although the two words are similar, the word "intention" is a better description of the quality that discriminates winning leaders, companies and brands. There's more sense of psychological commitment in the idea.

Another way to describe these organizations is that they have a "soul." Soulfulness implies unwavering adherence to inner principles and values. Within the soulful people we meet and the soulful enterprises we touch, there's an authentic commitment born of deep standards and ideals. They are guided by a clear and resolute point of view.

While all brands stand for something, conviction-fired brands stand *up* for something. Like great leaders, they are powered by incisive opinions. There's a philosophy that directs their actions. Not only do they have a profession; they have something they profess.

This is the prerequisite for any enterprise seeking to attain the peak of purposeful performance. In the businesses where purpose leads to breakthrough, there's a genuine intentionality — a clear-cut point of view that's passionately embraced inside.

To illustrate the differences, let's look at the two flagships of the sharing economy: Uber and Airbnb.

Uber set out to revolutionize the ride-hailing industry. But beyond that drive for category disruption, it's hard to find a "soul" within the business and the brand. There's no galvanizing point of view about life and the world.

On top of that void — or perhaps related to it — Uber's workplace culture became menacingly unhinged in spots. An internal audit led by former U.S. Attorney General Eric Holder concluded that the company's operating values — which included "toe-stepping" and "principled confrontation"—needed serious revamping.[9] At the same time, customers recoiled at executive actions that sometimes seemed dirty and gruff. Months of firings, resignations, CEO hiring struggles, lawsuits, a concealed data hack, a federal bribery probe, and allegations of abusive drivers have tarnished the company's reputation. As a result, the brand's logo bears a bit of resemblance to the Death Star, and the brand has steadily lost share to Lyft.[10]

Take an Uber over to Airbnb and you see a very different scene. In most reviews, Airbnb's business, culture and brand all get five-star ratings. At the root of it all, the company exhibits a conviction-powered "soul."

In a two-minute identity video, the company frames its corporate concept in this way:

> The world is full of cities and towns, constantly growing larger.
> But the people within them are less connected.
> Yet we are all yearning for a sense of place.
> We are all seeking to belong.
> We all want to connect and share, to feel accepted and feel safe.
> Imagine having that anywhere.
> Airbnb stands for something much bigger than travel.
> We imagine a world where you can belong anywhere.[11]

On the company website, co-founder and CEO Brian Chesky writes, "At the heart of our mission is the idea that people are fundamentally good and every community is a place where you can belong."[12] The company's stated purpose is to "create a world where everyone can 'belong anywhere.'"

The ideal of belonging gives a distinct shape to Airbnb's organizational culture. Meeting rooms in the company's San Francisco offices are designed to look and feel like a home. Each conference room is a representation of an actual host property, and a spate of "landing zones" (instead of offices) aims to ensure that employees can "belong anywhere" within the headquarters. Diversity and inclusion are core values of the "Airfam"—as the company calls its workforce—and everyone stays connected through biweekly, live-streamed world meetings and an annual, all-company conference called "One Airbnb." In each of the regional offices, a "ground control" team makes sure employees regularly connect around birthday celebrations and holiday events.[13]

The company's point of view about belonging shapes the external experience of the brand as well. Its looped, love-infused logo (which it calls the "Bélo") is a symbol of belonging, and its corporate tagline is "Belong Anywhere." Asserting its commitment to inclusion, the company requires all of its hosts and users to sign a pledge against discrimination.

At times, the company's fervent point of view has led it to take high-profile political stands. One of the most significant acts came in response to President Donald Trump's travel ban. CEO Brian Chesky told *Fortune*, "The notion that you wouldn't accept somebody from a country because of who they are, is just in complete violation of all the values that we believe."[14]

In response to the ban, Chesky offered free housing to refugees caught in limbo. Days later, the company hurriedly crafted an ad called "We Accept" and aired it during the Super Bowl. Featuring a montage of diverse faces, it proclaimed, "We believe no matter who you are, where you're from, who you love or who you worship, we all belong." Its hashtag — #weaccept — topped the trending list during the Super Bowl, and while not without some political controversy, the ad earned the brand a net bump in customer goodwill.

Inspired by a world where people can "belong anywhere," the company has expanded its offerings beyond 'homes for hire' to include 'experiences to acquire.' Airbnb customers can participate in a French cheese tasting in Paris or a sacred tattoo ceremony in Bangkok. Through a partnership with Resy (a restaurant reservation app), Airbnb users can also research and reserve places to eat during their travels.

To promote its offerings, the company has developed a number of corporate partnerships. But rather than selecting just anyone, it prioritizes a strong values match. One valued partner is *National Geographic* magazine. In 2017, the two brands capitalized on the cultural attention surrounding the total solar eclipse, which both viewed to be a reminder of our shared humanity. Together, they co-promoted a contest for a chance to stay at a geodesic dome in a remote location in Oregon. The stay was hosted by famed astrophysicist Jedidah Isler and included a private flight along the path of the eclipse.

Different than Uber, Airbnb is a company with "soul." Its enterprise is powered by a life-level point of view, and that soul power fuels its success. Ten years after its start-up, Airbnb operates in 190 countries and has hosted more than three hundred million guest visits.[15] In 2017, the company blew past its internal forecasts, posting almost $100 million in profit on $2.6 billion in revenue.[16]

Another icon of genuine intentionality is Starbucks. Although the company has taken some lumps at times, there's no denying that the coffee giant represents one of the greatest business and brand successes of our time. It has commanded its category for 25 years, and to note, that category is as "commoditized" as categories get. In world markets, coffee is the second-most traded commodity following crude oil. Despite the ubiquity of available coffee products and retail outlets, Starbucks lovers remain deeply loyal to their brand.

There are many factors that have contributed to Starbucks' rise and dominance, but a unique point of view is certainly one of them. In his book *The Starbucks Story,* author John Simmons writes, "At Starbucks . . . there is an almost tangible sense that the people and the company's 'friends' are united by a common outlook on life: one to do with embracing, not resenting, the tolerant opportunities of a broader view of life . . ."[17] The company's stated purpose is to "inspire and nurture the human spirit."

That philosophical orientation and sense of purpose stems from former CEO Howard Schultz's view of his late father and the work-related hardship his father endured. The senior Schultz held a variety of blue-collar jobs, most often as a truck driver. Despite working hard — sometimes taking on two or three jobs at a time — he always struggled financially. More significantly, crummy jobs squelched his spirit. They sapped his dignity and esteem.

Driven by a conviction that people should be treated well, Howard Schultz built a company that is progressive in its approach to employees, or "partners" as it prefers to call them. It offers all full- and part-time partners the opportunity to receive robust healthcare benefits and stock options. Through an association with Arizona State University, it also offers all its partners — 70 percent of whom are pre-college Gen Y and Zers — two years of college tuition-free. And in March 2018, the company announced that, after years of committed focus, it had eliminated all pay inequities in the U.S. due to race or gender.[18]

Another manifestation of the company's focus on human dignity is its commitment to ethical sourcing. Starbucks has invested more than $100 million into efforts to improve the livelihood of coffee farmers. It provides financing to farmers and support centers for sharing tools and best practices.[19]

Starbucks strives to treat its customers with a similar depth of dignity. Schultz famously said, "We're not in the coffee business serving people, we're in the people business, serving coffee."[20] The company's employee handbook instructs its baristas to be welcoming, be considerate and be involved. If you're a regular, your barista likely knows you by name and knows your standard order.

For the customer, this contributes to a feeling of connection. Connection was at the core of Howard's concept for the company: a "third place" between home and work where people could meet. Here's how Schultz described the business idea and its inception:

I was sent to Italy on a trip for Starbucks and came back with this feeling that the business Starbucks was in was the wrong business. What I wanted to bring back was the daily ritual and the sense of community and the idea that we could build this third place between home and work in America. It was an epiphany. I was out of my mind. I walked in [to a small coffee bar in Milan] and saw this symphony of activity, and the romance and the theater of coffee. And coffee being at the center of conversation, creating a sense of community. That is what spoke to me.[21]

Still today, the company views its stores as gathering hubs and cultivates communing. (*See its "Meet Me at Starbucks" campaign.*) A new, high-end "roastery" concept — a kind of taproom for coffee lovers — is the latest manifestation. "Starbucks coffee is exceptional, yes, but *emotional connection* is our true value proposition," says Schultz.[22]

Like Airbnb, Starbucks is a company with a "soul." It's fueled by a life-level point of view and a vision for how the world should be. The words articulated in the company's purpose statement — "to inspire and nurture the human spirit" — are more than a platitude; they represent a heartfelt devotion.

Life-Level Aims

As the Airbnb and Starbucks examples illustrate, the strongest points of view relate to deep human motivations. They reflect states of being that people really care about, like being accepted and feeling connected to others. Life-level stuff like that is worth getting out of bed and going to battle for.

Every business can put itself in a humanistic frame, and the best ones do. Disney isn't just in the entertainment business; it's in the happiness business. Nike isn't just in the athletic apparel business; it's in the human potential business. Yeti isn't just in the cooler business; it's in the adventure business.

Great businesses put themselves
in a humanistic frame.

Connecting your business to a big, universal motivation is the most effective way to drive engagement, relevance, and growth. Because it's bigger than either the business or the customer, it becomes a point of shared passion.

A great story of humanistic reframing came out of the war in Iraq. Following the U.S. invasion in 2003, the Army established its famed Camp Liberty base, and like every other base, there was a mess hall. It was called the Pegasus Grill, and it was under the command of a 25-year vet named Floyd Lee. Although Lee and his team received the same supplies as other mess halls did – uninspiring food stocks and standard-issue accoutrements – they transformed the dining experience into a culinary delight. They marinated the ribs, decked out the space, and gave mouthwatering names to the fare. It was an appealing attraction in the desert that soldiers drove miles to enjoy. What drove Floyd Lee was a reframing of his work. "As I see it, I am not just in charge of foodservice," he said. "I am in charge of morale."[23]

In a similar way, IKEA's approach to home furnishings is fueled by a humanistic ideal. The company has built an enviable brand and income statement on the Swedish ideal of egalitarianism. Its advertised point of view is: "all homes are created equal" and "better homes create a better society."

Speaking about his business concept, the late founder, Ingvar Kamprad, once said:

All nations and societies in both the East and West spend a disproportionate amount of their resources on satisfying a minority of the population. In our line of business, for example, far too many of the fine designs and new ideas are reserved for a small circle of the affluent. That situation has influenced the formulation of our objectives.[24]

Stemming from that worldview, IKEA's stated purpose is "to create a better everyday life for the many people." Its operating values include togetherness, humbleness, simplicity and cost-consciousness, and the company intentionally hires "down-to-earth, straight-forward people."[25]

Inside IKEA, egalitarianism can be seen in a variety of organizational features, like minimal hierarchy and humble job titles. The company provides full benefits for all part-time workers and has offered domestic partner benefits for over two decades. The town square of its Älmhult-based headquarters is an area called the Democratic Design Center.

Everyone at IKEA, from the Democratic Design Center on out, works to provide well-functioning, stylish furnishings at prices that all people can afford. The company continues to open new stores, driving volumes up so costs can go down. And its product innovations democratize home fashion trends.

Turning to the apparel industry, the Carhartt brand frames its business around the ideal of hard work. Born in Detroit, its working-class roots included the manufacture of overall bibs for railroad workers. The brand's purpose is to "serve and protect hardworking people." (*See Carhartt's manifesto in Appendix D.*) Chief Brand Officer Tony Ambroza told *Esquire*, "We stand for hard work. We've stood for that since 1889 when [Hamilton Carhartt] was focused on making a better product for workers that didn't get a better product. Times will come and go, times will change, but we've consistently stood with the working class."

Using an in-house marketing agency, the brand's marketing materials feature "real people doing real work." Its product offerings include "the hardest working t-shirts of all-time." The company's recruiting materials tout the value of hard work, and its philanthropic endeavors focus on trades workshops and work training for veterans.

Even as work and leisure are becoming more high-tech, Carhartt is thriving as a beacon for a blue-collar, DIY ideal. At a time when many brick-and-mortar apparel stores are closing, Carhartt continues to expand its presence. According to Ambroza, the brand is in a growth period.[26]

At Carhartt, the brand's system of thinking and all of its business activities are fueled by, and geared toward, the ideal of hard work. At IKEA, that ideal is egalitarianism – a better home life for all. Within Airbnb, it's belonging. At Starbucks, it's connection. These singular motivations are the human-centered guideposts – the highest-order aims – that inspire and direct all business proceedings. Importantly, each motivation inscribes an enterprise's distinct point of view.

Unique Angles on Life

So what is the set of universal human motivations? What makes one point of view different from another? And, when an enterprise adopts a particular ideal, what does it inherently oppose?

The answers lie in the physical structure of our brain. The very form of our gray matter gives us a map to the big human universals and the built-in polarities that explain different points of view. And conveniently enough, that structure resembles a compass.

Using the metaphor of a compass, here are the basic neurological functions of the different parts of the brain, expressed as "cardinal directions."

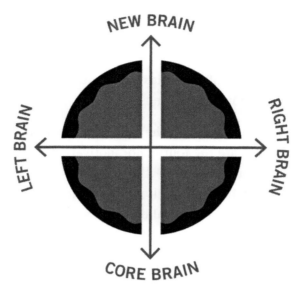

- The west represents our *left brain*. The left hemisphere of the human brain has a facility for logic, process and detail. It builds "monosemantic" models, meaning it ascribes single meanings to stimulus and sorts concepts into defined categories. It experiences reality through the lens of pre-determinism: causal relationships and linear sequences.[27]

- On the opposite pole, the east represents our *right brain*. The right hemisphere of the brain is more "polysemantic": intuitive, holistic and conceptual. It sparks to external stimuli and lights up in new environments – connecting to others, linking complex ideas and entertaining multiple meanings. It experiences reality through the lens of figurative associations and possibilities.[28]

- The north represents the cerebral cortex at the top of our brain. It's sometimes called the *new brain,* because it's the most recent evolutionary addition. It's where conscious thought happens, and it directs our voluntary actions.

- On the opposite pole, the south represents our *core brain* — the limbic system at the base of the brain. From an evolutionary standpoint, it's the oldest part of our circuitry. It's the home of memories and emotions and is the master of regulation and routine.

Using those "poles" as the basic structure of our mental compass, below are the four major motivational systems — the fundamental "orientations" — that we all possess. In study after study and model after model, neuropsychologists and behavioral scientists repeatedly validate these general drivers, even if the names are sometimes different.

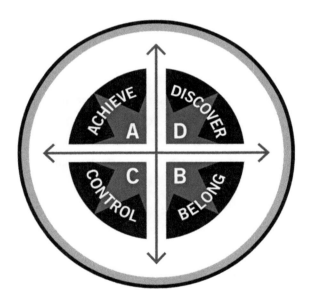

The Point of View Compass

A. The northwest quadrant is the domain of *achievement*. It reflects the human drive to enhance our individual condition, and it was wired into us by the "survival of the fittest" mandate that guided our evolution. In this motivational mode, we seek progress, set goals, take action and compete with others and ourselves. We solve problems and measure concrete impacts.

B. On the opposite pole from "A," the southeast quadrant is the domain of *belonging*. While "A" prioritizes the success of "me," this quadrant is all about "we" — interdependence over independence. It's a byproduct of our tribal ancestry and our evolutionary success as social beings. In our drive to create and support interpersonal bonds, we seek group acceptance, cultivate closeness, and create cultural norms.

C. The southwest quadrant is the domain of *control*. In a world of chaos and disorder, we have a drive to regulate, plan, and organize. We create systems, follow procedures, and execute with excellence.

D. On the opposite pole from "C," the northeast quadrant is the domain of *discovery and experience*. While "C" prioritizes order and routine, this quadrant is all about change and stimulation. We seek out new insights, new concepts, and stimulating experiences.

Beyond just naming the four universal motivations that drive us, the most important feature of this "navigational tool" is the relativity it depicts. Ideals never exist in isolation. They can only be understood within a field of contrasting alternatives. As the Point of View Compass implies, there's always an inherent tension vs. the opposing point of view.

With this lens, you can begin to see meaningful differences in the points of view of the people you know. As it turns out, we all have an innate leaning, a values preference, a core motivation that we're more heavily pulled toward. As an illustration, the table below shows how prototypical personality types map to the four quadrants.

	A Achieve	B Belong	C Control	D Discover & Experience
Primary Focus	what	who	how, where and when	why
Archetypal Personas*	warriors, champions, rebels, daredevils	regular folk, jokesters, lovers, caregivers	guardians, rulers, craftsmen, connoisseurs	idealists, dreamers, explorers, masterminds
Famous Figures	Alexander the Great, Serena Williams, Richard Branson	Dalai Lama, Blake Shelton, Ellen DeGeneres	Coco Chanel, Martha Stewart, Simon Cowell	Leonardo da Vinci, Walt Disney, Amelia Earhart
Dominant Qualities	results-driven, measures-focused, competitive, bold, persistent, risk-taking, decisive	caring, casual, consensus-driven, welcoming, humble, loyal, empathetic, supportive	stable, respectful, committed, meticulous, methodical, realistic, cautious	inventive, free-spirited, open-minded, creative, playful, inquisitive, expressive

Note: For a deep dive on archetypes, read the essential guide by Margaret Mark and Carol Pearson: The Hero and the Outlaw.

What makes the famous figures above so iconic is the clarity and coherence of their points of view. They define a universal motivation, and they do so unapologetically. Aiding that clarity and coherence is the fact that, for each type of persona, there is a definitive "point of opposition."

Because the four fundamental orientations exist in the general population, there are four broad audience types within the consumer marketplace. That's why a needs-based segmentation of any given category will typically generate four groupings with segment names resembling the ones below.

	A Achieve	B Belong	C Control	D Discover & Experience
Sample Segment Names	strivers achievers aspirers	bonders connectors harmonizers	perfectionists pragmatists traditionalists	experiencers creatives seekers

Turning now to businesses, the quadrants also provide a lens for understanding the points of view of different brands. Here are four illustrations:

A. Nike typifies an "A" (Achieve) orientation. The company is named for the Greek goddess of victory, and it aligns itself with the world's most prominent champions – from Michael Jordan to Rory McIlroy. With its "Just Do It" tagline and campaigns like "Find Your Greatness," it inspires and enables the athlete in all of us. Note that Nike inherently opposes acceptance of the status quo, an ideal that resides in opposite quadrant B.

B. Swirled with hippy love, Ben & Jerry's is aligned with the "B" (Belong) quadrant. The peace sign it displays is a symbol of its point of view, and the brand advances its social agenda with special flavors like "Bob Marley's One Love" and "Hubby Hubby" (in support of gay marriage). Charming, cheeky, and deliciously creamy, the brand is enjoyably welcoming to all. Note that the brand's interdependent mindset is inherently at odds with quadrant A, where individual drive reigns supreme.

C. With its focus on craftsmanship, Hermès has a "C" (Control) orientation. Former chairman Jean-Louis Dumas said, "The world is divided into two: those who know how to use tools, and those who do not."[29] Instead of playing on glitz and trends, Hermès focuses on meticulous production. The humble tools of its trade are wax, awls, needles, and mallets. Every Birkin bag is stitched by hand and can take 15 to 23 hours to make.[30] By contrast, glitz and trends (the pursuit of the shiny and new) belong in the opposite quadrant D.

D. We can see a strong "D" (Discover and Experience) orientation in a Brazilian cosmetics brand called Quem Disse, Berenice? – the name is slang for "Who says I have to?" The stores are vibrantly colorful, and its flamboyant products challenge the norms of makeup. They include an orange lipstick and a metallic green eye pencil. It's not uncommon to see a sales associate wearing competing shades on her eyes and lips. Through its marketing events, Quem Disse, Berenice? invites women to swap out an old lipstick and try a bright new color. This point of view stands in stark contrast to the exactness and order that's valued by quadrant C.

When a brand has a point of view, it inherently aligns itself with a group of values cohorts, and those values cohorts are instinctively drawn to the brand. They forge a relationship based on shared motivations. They are "soul" mates.

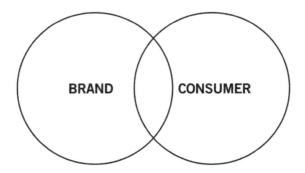

Brands and consumers align around shared motivations.

For consumers, what's at play here is a psychological principle called "confirmation bias." As humans, we like to be with like-minded people, and we embrace points of view that are aligned with our own. It gives us a sense of identity and connection.

So it is that audiences and brands tend to sync up along motivational grounds – finding a common home in one of the four quadrants of the Point of View Compass. Because of this phenomenon, we can observe natural distinctions and delineations within categories. In the table below, I've shown how the brands in three familiar categories occupy different motivational spaces, aligning themselves with a different values cohort group.

	A Achieve	B Belong	C Control	D Discover & Experience
Sample Segment Names	strivers achievers aspirers	bonders connectors harmonizers	perfectionists pragmatists traditionalists	experiencers creatives seekers
Cars	BMW	Subaru	Mercedes- Benz	Jeep
Sportswear	Nike	Russell Athletic	Lacoste	Adidas
Insurance	Liberty Mutual	State Farm	USAA	Zurich

In the next chapter, you will use the Point of View Compass as a "navigational tool" to help you define your convictions, values and purpose. It will allow you to identify:

- Where the primary motivation of your brand lies – its prevailing orientation
- The primary force of opposition that your brand pushes against

- Which audience type your brand most closely aligns with
- How your governing philosophy differs from those of your competitors

Case for Action

- Today's most successful businesses and brands display an impassioned point of view. Compared to other "purpose-driven" organizations, brands with a point of view have higher-octane fuel in the purpose tank. That's because they have life-level convictions that *precede* their purpose. Their sense of purpose is conviction-inspired — the activation of a heartfelt devotion.
- The strongest points of view reflect a fundamental human motivation and the inherent polarity that motivation represents: individualistic achievement vs. communal belonging; unrestrained discovery vs. ordered control.
- Brands and consumers align around shared motivations.

Actions to Take

- Use the Point of View Compass to identify where your brand's primary motivation lies, how it aligns with a core audience, and how that orientation differs from those of your competitors.

CHAPTER 2
Craft Your Creed

This above all: to thine own self be true.

—Shakespeare, Hamlet, Act 1, Scene 2

The Elements of a Creed

To capture your brand's point of view and intention, you need to set your mind to philosophy and your pen to paper and create a creed. A creed — or credo — is a "codification of belief or opinion." An example is the Universal Declaration of Human Rights that was adopted by the U.N. General Assembly in 1948. Among its thirty articles are the convictions that "all human beings are born free and equal in dignity and rights," "everyone has the right to education," and "no one shall be held in slavery or servitude."

Although the notion of "why" is often shorthanded to mean purpose, a complete "why" — a robust brand creed — actually has three parts: purpose, prime value, and convictions.

With these three elements, you can effectively codify your brand's point of view — its unique outlook, its central motivation and intention.

★

PURPOSE

PRIME VALUE

CONVICTIONS

As an organizing framework, the creed captures the governing philosophy of your organization and your brand. Within that framework, purpose is the key "action item," and the prime value and convictions articulate the underlying devotion.

A creed codifies your brand's point of view.
Purpose is the key "action item."

Convictions

Starting at the foundation of the creed framework, your brand's convictions are nothing more — and nothing less — than its deeply held beliefs, the ideas it holds to be true. Within them resides a vision for how people, life or the world should be.

A conviction is a deeply held belief –
an idea your brand holds to be true.

A conviction typically starts with the words "I (or we) believe" or can be readily expressed in that form. The discriminating quality is the feeling of being sure, almost as if the idea has been proven. A well-known benchmark appears in the Declaration of Independence, where the Founding Fathers pronounced: "We hold these truths to be self-evident, that all men are created equal, that they are endowed by their Creator with certain unalienable Rights, that among these are Life, Liberty and the pursuit of Happiness."

As a brand, your convictions are your fuel source. They convey your sense of devotion and vision and empower your organization with the courage of truth. They are the blood supply to the heart of your purpose.

Examples:

- **Barbie:** We believe that a little girl can be anything she wants to be.
- **MGM:** We believe mankind was not meant to be bored.

- **Dove:** We believe that beauty should be a source of confidence, and not anxiety.

Prime Value

Values are what one holds to be most important. Through an accumulation of experiences — starting with its founding — your brand and organization hold certain ideas to be inalienable. These are its values. They are properties or qualities of inherent worth, like empathy, integrity, and expertise. They are always one-word nouns.

Human values align with the motivations in the Point of View Compass. Because we're driven to achieve, we value courage. Because we desire belonging, we value harmony. Because we seek control, we value predictability. Because we're motivated to discover, we value exploration.

The table below shows a sample set of values, aligned to the four quadrants of the compass. A more comprehensive listing of human values appears in Appendix A.

	A Achieve	B Belong	C Control	D Discover & Experience
Primary Focus	what	who	how, where and when	why
Sample Values	performance courage progress ambition determination	benevolence harmony cooperation humor equality	integrity discipline reliability competence security	creativity knowledge optimism imagination exploration

Note that all values are not created equal. According to values experts like Milton Rokeach, there are two types: "end" values and "means" values. The former describes a preferential state of being; the latter describes a mode of conduct for achieving the end value. I'll discuss the application of means values in a moment. For now, let's focus on end values.

While the Point of View Compass is about general direction, operating with true conviction requires that you have a specific bearing — a precise angle on the world, the equivalent of Airbnb's belonging and Starbucks' connection. For IKEA, it's egalitarianism.

Of all your values, this is the predominant one — your central human aim, your prime directive, your prime value. A prime value defines the ultimate aim of endeavor, the end state the enterprise desires for people and the world. It is the "heart" of the brand or company purpose. It answers the question, "To what end?"

A prime value defines your brand's central human aim.

For a large business that wants to get larger, this degree of singularity can feel confining; but in the point-of-view business, decisiveness is critical. And from a management perspective, it's a powerful tool. Howard Schultz writes, "I have long believed in the power of a word or a single phrase to effectively communicate a business imperative — and to inspire people. The best words are never big or complicated, but are packed with emotion and meaning, leaving no question of what I expect of myself and others."[1]

To describe the power of focus, famed pastor Rick Warren uses the metaphor of light. In *The Purpose-Driven Life,* he writes, "Diffused light has little power or impact, but you can concentrate its energy by focusing it. With a magnifying glass, the rays of the sun can be focused to set grass or paper on fire. When light is focused even more as a laser beam, it can cut through steel."[2]

The prime value is reminiscent of the "Commander's Intent"

that's used in the U.S. Army. When preparing for a military operation, the top brass declares the desired end state, the "prime directive." Then the staff and subordinates go to work to establish action plans and orders.

Singularity is important from a branding perspective as well. When marketing a brand, most strategists advocate for single-mindedness. That's because, according to marketing scientists like Byron Sharp, share grows as "mental availability" grows. When a brand represents a clear, singular motivation — the way Airbnb, Starbucks, IKEA, and Carhartt do — consumers can more easily access and imprint its meaning.

A prime value tells your organization what is most important when all is said and done. It is the beacon for your product experience, the essence of your brand's meaning and your central point of advocacy. It is the soul of your brand's purpose.

Examples:

- **Barbie:** Potential
- **MGM:** Excitement
- **Dove:** Self-esteem

Purpose

As I described in the Introduction, a purpose is the business's inspirational 'reason for being' beyond making money. It's the definitive difference your organization seeks to make in the world. It's what your underlying point of view calls your organization to do.

While strategies must continually evolve, purpose is more timeless. That's not to say it's eternal, but it should be big enough that the organization's work is never really done. While leaders come and go, competitive context changes and markets shift, purpose should be a steadfast lighthouse beckoning progress.

With your convictions stated and prime value defined, purpose turns the underlying point of view into an activist statement of intent. It propels your organization forward, in the direction of your prime value.

Examples:

- **Barbie:** We exist to inspire and nurture the limitless possibilities of girls.

- **MGM:** We exist to blow the mind of all mankind.

- **Dove:** We exist to help more women feel beautiful every day.

PURPOSE
To bring the gift of health to life

PRIME VALUE
Vitality

CONVICTIONS

We believe that energy and vitality
fuel the pursuit of happiness.

We believe that our world of plenty
is creating a poverty of health.

We believe that good health
should be within reach of all.

We believe that complete nutrition
is not about quick fixes.

We believe that you can't have
trust without truth.

Sample Creed
Here is an illustration
of the fully formed
output. It is the creed
for one of my clients:
Pharmavite, the maker of
Nature Made vitamins.

Operating Values

Although operating values aren't one of the three basic elements of a creed, they are a necessary addendum for a corporate brand or autonomous branded house. That's because an essential component of a company's identity is how its employees comport themselves and perform their work. Operating values describe that "code of conduct." They are the standards by which employees are measured. As such, they represent a critical opportunity to support and enable your convictions and purpose.

Operating values define how employees should comport themselves and perform their work.

Recall from earlier that there are two types of values: "end" values and "means" values. Means values describe a mode of conduct for achieving the end value. That is to say, operating values support delivery of the prime value.

Example: The U.S. Army's "Seven Core Values"

- Loyalty – Bear true faith and allegiance to the U.S. Constitution, the Army, your unit and other soldiers

- Duty – Fulfill your obligations

- Respect – Treat people as they should be treated

- Selfless service – Put the welfare of the nation, the Army and your subordinates before your own

- Honor – Live up to all the Army values

- Integrity – Do what's right, legally and morally

- Personal courage – Face fear, danger or adversity

The Process

In the frenzy of day-to-day business, it's hard to give time and mental focus to philosophy, but in a conviction-fueled enterprise, the creed is everything – the fount from which all activity flows. As inspiration for making that "spiritual investment," consider these cases of great, soulful enterprises:

- The words that launched America — the Declaration of Independence — were developed over the course of 24 days. They were first drafted by a "Committee of Five" — with Thomas Jefferson as the lead writer — and then debated and revised by the full Continental Congress.

- In 1976, IKEA founder Ingvar Kamprad spent days putting his governing philosophy into a treatise. His thirteen-page "Testament of a Furniture Dealer" is the creed that has guided the company's extraordinary global growth. In 1996, Ingvar added "A Little IKEA Dictionary" at the end, noting, "Words are an important part of the IKEA heritage."[3]

- Patagonia's "philosophies" were born in 1991, after a dozen of the company's leaders went for a walkabout in the real Patagonia in Argentina. As they meandered, they reflected on the company's unique convictions and values, and upon their return, ecologist and author Jerry Mander captured their conclusions in writing.

The process of identifying and codifying your creed proceeds through the following steps:

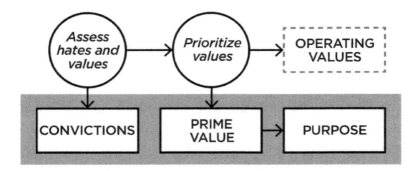

Assessing Hates and Values

Your brand, like every business, has unique "truths" that underlie it; but often, those truths haven't been expressly identified. The power of a point of view can't be unleashed until you've taken that step — until the governing ideas are made explicit.

Socrates advised his students, "Know thyself; know your strengths and weaknesses; your relation to the universe; your potentialities; your spiritual heritage; your aims and purposes; take stock of thyself." That's the mindset that must govern the development of your creed. As a brand, it's all too easy to lose your identity by looking outward — following competitive benchmarks instead of remaining true to your own.

The root of the word "authentic" comes from Socrates' native Greek language. It derives from the word "authentes," which in the original Greek meant "acting on one's own authority." That's the holy grail of purpose hunting: a source of innate authority. In the words of Tom's of Maine cofounder Tom Chappell: "Success means never letting the competition define you. Instead, you have to define yourself based on a point of view you care deeply about."[4]

A point of view is always found within. It's never invented; it's always unearthed. That's because, by definition, it's *self-evident*. It reflects truths that have been acquired through experience. As author-philosopher Wayne Dyer said, "A belief system is nothing more than a thought you've thought over and over again."[5]

Excavating Heritage

Perhaps the most clever and important line on this subject comes from author Joey Reiman, who asserts, "The fruits are in the roots."[6] Indeed, a lot is illuminated by the origin story of a business. In the same way that a person's personality is evident in his or her youth, the core DNA of an enterprise was imprinted at its inception.

An inspiring example can be found in KIND Snacks. The "soul" of that brand originated in a Nazi concentration camp. The father of founder Daniel Lubetzky was a Holocaust survivor and told his son a story of wartime kindness. While his father was imprisoned and starving in Dachau, a German soldier tossed a potato at his feet while no one was looking. Growing up with that story in his heart profoundly shaped Daniel's values. He says, "Kindness is really magical, because it's one of the only forces in nature that can just create happiness without any additional money or inputs. All you have to do is sincerely want to help someone else."[7]

To find your brand's "authentes," start by digging into the head and heart of the founder.

- What was his or her personal background? How did up-bringing, environment, religion, etc. shape his or her motivations?

- What was his or her personality like? What was his or her general outlook and temperament? What traits did he or she admire in others? What kinds of people were in his or her inner circle?

- What's the story of how the business got started? What was the original 'big idea?' What was the need behind it? What was the wrong he or she wanted to right? What was his or her vision for how people, life or the world should be?

- What were the values that guided the early operations?

- Why the brand name and original iconography (symbols, colors, imagery)? What were the intended meanings?

- What were the original promotional messages?

"Authentes" in a New-to-the-World Business

If you're starting a new business, you're building your heritage myth now. Make your governing motivations explicit by exploring the same lines of inquiry: How did your parents, upbringing, environment, religion, etc. shape your point of view? And how is that point of view shaping the concept of your business?

Assessing the Culture

Once you've resurrected the full plot of the origin story, layer on a study of the organizational culture as it stands today.

- Which of the original traits and motivations have endured over time?

- What artifacts of the heritage are most readily observable today? What are the dominant stories that endure?

- What are the qualities of people who succeed in the current organization?

- What values and behaviors are most rewarded?

- What behaviors and attitudes are most rejected?

- In recent years, when was the company at its best? What were the dynamics at play?

Here, it can be helpful to engage your frontline employees. Not only will it get you closer to the "truth," the very act of soliciting input will facilitate buy-in to the final product. This can be done through interviews, focus groups, or a survey. Using an intranet forum, IBM conducted a 72-hour "Values Jam." A more low-tech way to do it: hang up easel sheets in a public space and ask people to provide their input.

It's also important to analyze the top boss. As the saying goes, culture starts at the top, and the personality of the executive suite can have a significant impact on norms and values. Consider his or her background, motivations, general outlook and temperament. How are his or her personal values impacting the culture?

From that multi-pronged assessment, look for key themes: recurring qualities, prevailing attitudes, underlying drivers, and inalienable codes. Take the example of Hershey. The founder, Milton Hershey, had a very big heart. He built and endowed an orphanage and was famous for saying, "One is only happy in proportion as he makes others feel happy." In the corporate culture of Hershey today, there's a related trait that people refer to as "Hershey nice." A general theme of warmth emerges from those codes. The brand's recent campaign is called "Heartwarming the World."

Mapping Out Your General Orientation

From your heritage and culture assessments, identify where your brand resides within the Point of View Compass: Achieve, Belong, Control, or Discover/Experience. What archetypal persona is your brand most like? What is the dominant motivation?

- If your brand and culture has an "A" orientation, it will tend to be results-driven, measures-focused, competitive, persistent, bold, risk-taking, and decisive.

- A brand and culture with a "B" orientation is more caring, casual, consensus-driven, welcoming, humble, loyal, empathetic, and supportive.

- A brand and culture with a "C" orientation is stable, respectful, committed, meticulous, methodical, realistic, and cautious about risk.

- A brand and culture with a "D" orientation tends to be more inventive, free-spirited, open-minded, creative, playful, inquisitive, and expressive.

One way to sharpen this view is to look for competitive distinctions. What archetypal personas are your competitors most like? What thinking styles dominate their actions? Look for clues in their messaging, offerings, and internal cultures.

Hates

Now that you've got a general bearing on your brand's point of view, it's time to start articulating an actual creed. That process starts in a contrary place: the conditions that your brand or company "hates." Knowing what you're "against" is the clearest way to determine what you're "for."

To have a clear and distinct point of view, you and your team must ask yourselves: What is the enemy we fight? Is there a particular injustice we see in the world? A societal or marketplace wrong? What attitudes or behaviors does the brand inherently reject? Abraham Lincoln hated the tyranny of oppression. Airbnb hates xenophobia. Patagonia hates environmental degradation. Red Bull hates limits. The people at Method cleaning products are "people against dirty." These "points of opposition" will point you toward the motivations that drive your brand.

Values

On the flipside of "hates" are values. Using the list in Appendix A, identify your brand's top five-to-seven values — ideals that emerged from your heritage and culture assessments and are consistent with your general compass bearing. As a

frame for selection, find words that best complete the following
sentences:

- To us, the world would be a better place if people experienced (or demonstrated) _____ more often.
- In the way we operate — or in the design of our offering
  — a condition or quality that's highly valued is _____.

In the upcoming exercises, you will use those values words
to articulate your convictions, purpose, and operating values.

Expressing Convictions

Convictions arise from the natural pairing of values and hates.
A given value isn't conviction-worthy unless it has a strong
"anti-value." Below are some examples of convictions, each
arising from a "hate" and a vision for how the world should be.

	Value *inferred*	Hate *inferred*	Conviction *stated*
The Washington Post	Enlightenment	Lack of information	We believe democracy dies in darkness.
Nike	Potential	Acceptance of status quo	We believe there is no finish line.
LPK Design	Courage	Playing it safe	We believe nothing of consequence happens without risk.
Apple	Simplicity	Complexity	We believe that simplicity is the ultimate sophistication.
Beech-Nut	Purity	Artificiality	We believe nature is always right.

To articulate your brand's convictions, start by pairing your
top values with opposing hates. Then, using each pair as a

springboard, craft statements of conviction. Here are some tips for writing effective convictions:

- ✔ Use the stem "we believe that." While not an absolute, that phrasing generally conveys more sense of "truth." By contrast, the stem "we believe in" connotes vague, generic advocacy.

- ✔ Telegraph what the enterprise is "against" − either overtly or indirectly.

- ✔ Avoid bland platitudes that are hard to disagree with, e.g., "We believe that all women are wonderful."

- ✔ Avoid statements that are internally focused or self-congratulatory, e.g., "We believe that we provide the best service."

A strong creed will typically contain three-to-five conviction statements, covering the range of both "ends" and "means" − both the high-level point of view and operational philosophy. Multiple statements are needed in order to articulate a comprehensive belief system, but beyond three to five, you start to lose the sense of definitive opinion.

A Prime Value and Purpose

Prime Value

To identify your prime value, go back to the list of your brand's top five-to-seven values, pulled from Appendix A. Which is the dominant one?

In making your selection, it's helpful to build a "values ladder." For example, Apple values both creativity and simplicity, but "creativity realized" is the company's end goal for anybody who uses its devices. In service of unlocking human creativity,

Apple designs for intuitive functionality. So simplicity is a means value.

When selecting your prime value, the key is to find the right, best rung on the values ladder. For many brands and companies, the prime value represents the desired end state. Zappos has succeeded by delivering happiness. Pirch (the high-end kitchen and bath retailer) is a purveyor of joy. 1-800-Flowers is a vessel for sympathy. Within Diageo's beer and spirits portfolio, Guinness pursues communion, Smirnoff advocates for inclusivity, and Johnnie Walker champions progress.[8]

For others – particularly those with a quadrant C ("how") orientation – the priority may be the means. At Hermès, craftsmanship rules. Whole Foods values interdependence. Carhartt has grown through hard work.

Another factor to consider is your core customers' motivations. The opportunity in a conviction-driven approach is to build a "movement" that actively involves and engages your customers. That requires that the end motivation be shared.

Ultimately, whether it's at the top of the ladder or lower down, you're trying to answer the following question: "At the heart of our brand's intentionality, what is the single most important thing?"

To help you sort through the available options, consider four lenses:

1. What is our organization genuinely passionate about? Beyond making money, what do we really care about? What is our principal "hate," and what value word is the antonym?

2. Philosophically speaking, what makes our brand unique relative to our competition? It may be an "end" ambition for how the enterprise wants to impact people's lives,

or it may be a "means" — mode of conduct — that it cares about deeply.

3. What do our core customers value?

4. What does the world most need?

Again, the goal is to identify one prime value — the ultimate aim of endeavor, the brand's singular motivation. This will be the basis for your purpose.

Purpose

The next step in the process is to articulate your brand's purpose statement. Below are several strong examples.

- American Red Cross: To enable Americans to perform extraordinary acts in the face of emergencies
- EY: To build a better work world
- LEGO: To inspire and develop the builders of tomorrow
- Lowe's: To help people love where they live
- SunTrust Bank: To light the way to financial well-being
- Wheaties: To fuel the champion within

A full listing of sample purpose statements appears in Appendix B.

To craft your purpose statement, simply turn your prime value into a statement of activist intent. As you do so, here are some criteria to follow:

✔ *Start with the stem "we exist to."* This creates the sense of *raison d'être*. And it cues a verb, thereby defining the entity in terms of action and activism.

✔ *Convey the prime value* — what the enterprise holds to be most important at the life level. The word itself doesn't need to appear, but the sensibility must be evident. This is how the enterprise's unique point of view comes to bear.

✔ *Put the business in service to people and the world.* While not mandatory, it can help to name the people you serve.

✔ *Build in a direct or implied connection to the category.* Make sure the purpose is sufficiently lofty, but not in the ether.

✔ *Be concise, and incorporate memorable language.* You don't want your associates to have to search for a document to retrieve the purpose. It should reside in the front of their minds and roll readily off their tongues.

✔ *Avoid the words "by" and "through."* Those are signals that you've incorporated a "what" or "how" in your purpose. Force yourself to be single-minded about "why."

✔ *Ensure the statement is sufficiently generative.* That is, does it inspire new and broader thinking about the business? Does it demand product or service innovation? Does it imply new forms of marketing engagement and social activism?

Operating Values

If your business is a corporate brand or autonomous branded house, go back to your original list of five-to-seven top values. What remains after selecting your prime value will be the basis for your operating values. Operating values always exist as a set, and in some organizations, the list can run as long as a dozen statements. But in general, seven is a good maximum; and recalling the metaphor of focused light, the tighter the list the better.

In terms of structure, operating values can be expressed using individual values words like the ones that appear in

Appendix A — words like diversity, responsibility, leadership, and collaboration. They can also be expressed as behaviors. For example, one of Method's "seven obsessions" is "care like crazy." The most effective approach combines the two — pairing the noun with a specific description of the desired behavior. Examples of operating values appear in Appendix C.

Another approach to operating values is to articulate them as "principles" — specific operating tenets by which the enterprise distinguishes itself in market and achieves marketplace success. The content depends on the business domain, but here are some illustrations:

- In its work and offerings, *The New York Times* seeks to "hold power to account" and "direct people's attention to things that matter."

- When it comes to its environmental practices, Burt's Bees is committed to "do as bees do." Since bees don't leave a footprint, neither does the company. Its stated policy is to send zero waste to landfill.

- In the "Green Apron" book that it provides to its baristas, Starbucks calls out the "Five Ways of Being." They include "be welcoming," "be considerate" and "be involved."

- Restaurant chain Sweetgreen publishes its "food ethos," which includes local sourcing, scratch cooking, and a transparent supply chain.

Adding Rhetorical and Visual Drama

Once you've defined the basic elements of your creed, a powerful way to bring it to life is through a written or video manifesto. Essentially, a manifesto is an executional vehicle for sharing your creed with your stakeholders, and it offers the opportunity to lift spirits with compelling verse and poetic imagery. As with the Declaration of Independence ("we hold these truths to be self-evident . . ."), rich, rallying language serves to embed the creed not only in people's minds, but also in their hearts. It also allows for some distinctive branding, like Pedigree's "Dogma" and Goldfish's "Manifishto." Examples of manifestos appear in Appendix D.

Although there's no formula for a manifesto, here's a general structure for crafting your narrative:

- The deep human context — presenting insight about universal motivations
- Relevant heritage "truths" — celebrating the brand's purposeful birthright
- Your convictions
- Your prime value and purpose
- Needs of the world that relate to the purpose and the company's intended actions to address them

Naturally, video can be a highly effective medium for presenting a manifesto. Publicly available examples include: MGM's "Welcome to the Show," L.L. Bean's "We Believe," Cincinnati Children's "Our Purpose," Harley-Davidson's "Live By It," The Clinton Foundation's "We're All in This Together," Johnson's Baby's "Choose Gentle," Southwest Airlines' "Our Purpose and Vision," Pedigree's "We're for Dogs," Jackson Hole's "Stay Wild," and a film called "Electric Cooperative Purpose" by the National Rural Electric Cooperative Association (NRECA).

In order to succeed in grabbing souls, your film must have superior production values: stirring photography, expressive music, and genuine humanity. A standard feature is the first-person plural point of view ("we"): of our people, by our people and for our people.

The "Five Opportunities" Revisited

In the Introduction, I talked about the "five opportunities of purpose": employee engagement, innovation generation, societal contribution, brand relevance, and consumer attention. As I hope I've demonstrated, the true power of purpose is unleashed when purpose is fueled by an underlying devotion: heartfelt convictions and a primary human motivation. These additional elements of creed are vital to the work of:

- Shaping an internal culture in which employees are aligned and engaged.

- Developing offerings that stretch the brand and foster emotional connection.

- Making a societal contribution that's truly meaningful.

- Building a brand identity that telegraphs the organization's driving intent.

- Making waves in the popular culture.

In the chapters that follow, I'll discuss the work of turning the five opportunities of purpose into realities. As I do so, I'll reference the broader concept of 'creed' to convey that more potent fuel source that powers success. While purpose is the beating heart, your prime value and convictions will be your blood supply.

Case for Action

- A creed captures your brand's point of view and intention. It has three elements: purpose, prime value, and convictions. Purpose is the critical "action item," and the prime value and convictions articulate the underlying devotion.

- Your brand's convictions are its deeply held beliefs – the ideas it holds to be true. They convey your sense of devotion and vision and empower your organization with the courage of certainty.

- Values are what one holds to be most important. Your brand's predominant value is its "prime value." It is the heart of your brand's purpose – the beacon for your product experience, the essence of your brand's meaning, and your central point of advocacy.

- Your brand's purpose is its inspirational 'reason for being.' It is a steadfast lighthouse beckoning progress. It propels your organization forward.

- For a corporate brand or autonomous branded house, operating values provide a "code of conduct" for employees. This represents a critical opportunity to support and enable the convictions and purpose.

Actions to Take

- Codify your brand's point of view in a creed framework.

- Assess your brand's "hates" and values by taking stock of the founder's motivations and the cultural DNA of the organization.

- Pair your top hates and values to form the basis for your belief system. For each pairing, articulate a "we believe" statement of conviction.

- Prioritize your values, choosing a prime value that answers the question: "At the heart of our brand's intentionality, what is the single most important thing?"

- Articulate a brand purpose by turning your prime value into a statement of activist intent ("we exist to").

- For a corporate brand or autonomous branded house, articulate your operating values.

- Bring your creed to life with a written or video manifesto, giving the content additional imagery and drama.

CHAPTER 3
Engage Your Organization

To move the world, we must first move ourselves.

—Socrates

Higher Meaning in Work

Following the Great Fire of London, England's preeminent architect, Sir Christopher Wren, was commissioned to rebuild 52 churches in the city, including his signature project: St. Paul's Cathedral. One day, as he surveyed the construction site, he came upon a sullen stonemason hammering a block of granite.

"What are you working on?" Wren asked. "I'm chipping this rock down to size," the laborer replied glumly, taking long pauses between each swing of his hammer. Continuing on, Wren came upon a second stonemason who was chipping away with a bit more vigor. Asked what he was doing, the worker replied, "I'm fashioning a part of the northeast wall." Minutes later, Wren encountered a third stonemason. This man displayed obvious enthusiasm for his vocation. He paid loving attention to his work product and swung his hammer fervently. Asked what he was doing, the mason replied, "I'm building a cathedral!"

The story of the stonemasons is often used to illustrate the motivating power of purpose – a reason to get out of bed in the morning. For as long as humankind has toiled, we've found inspiration and energy in the higher meaning of work. A related story recounts President Kennedy's visit to NASA in 1962. Encountering a janitor in the hallway, Kennedy asked the man about the nature of his work. The custodian replied, "Well, Mr. President, I'm helping to put a man on the moon."

Into present times – and especially in present times – a critical opportunity of purpose is employee engagement. Purpose gives meaning to work and inspires excellence and creativity. As Daniel Pink discovered in *Drive: The Surprising Truth about What Motivates Us,* "The most deeply motivated people – not to mention those who are most productive and satisfied – hitch their desires to a cause larger than themselves."[1]

In its 2016 "Putting Purpose to Work" report, PricewaterhouseCoopers (PwC) found that 83 percent of employees say that purpose in the workplace adds meaning to day-to-day work, and 53 percent say it energizes them.[2] According to the IBM Smarter Workforce Institute, 80 percent of employees have a positive work experience when their work is aligned with their organization's core values.[3] And The Energy Project, in collaboration with *Harvard Business Review*, found that employees are 177 percent more likely to stay with an organization when they derive a higher level of meaning from work.[4]

Building a Meaning-Filled Culture

To create a meaningful experience for your employees, you have to create a meaning-filled culture. You don't just roll out a purpose and suddenly get engaged employees. It takes a lot of hard work and sustained effort. Think of it as an ongoing workout to grow the size and shape of your organization's heart. Essentially, you're building a corporate body that "bleeds your creed."

Although the effort required can seem daunting, the rewards are great. The evidence suggests that the more deeply and broadly your workforce holds a common belief system, the more likely it is that the organization will perform at a high level. That was the discovery of Harvard professors John Kotter and James Heskett in their study on *Corporate Culture and Performance*. They found that firms that have cultures based on shared values outperform companies that don't. Their revenues grew four times faster, and stock prices grew twelve times faster.[5] Another study, cited by executive search firm Spencer Stuart, showed that "the extent to which employees align with an organization's culture (explains) as much as 25 percent of performance variance."[6]

During my time at P&G, I saw this firsthand on the Pampers brand. In the 2000s, the business orchestrated a remarkable turnaround by building a baby-passionate culture. Bucking P&G's standard templates, the brand adopted its own high ideal, as well as its own hiring criteria – prioritizing love for babies and zeal for their development. The team also transformed its office environment, turning it into a baby-centric romper zone. It included onsite daycare, portraits of employees with their babies, and oversized furniture that encouraged employees to see the world through a baby's eyes. That internal transformation drove external actions that added billions to the topline.

In high-performing cultures, the employees all care about the same thing. They see the world through the same filter. They have unified convictions that maximize the output of their collective energies. As Peter Drucker once observed, "The most successful company is not the one with the most brains, but the most brains acting in concert."[7]

One of the most telegraphic examples is Patagonia. For the better part of forty years, the outdoor-apparel company has sustained a growth rate well above industry averages.[8] Behind that success is a well-defined culture that stems directly from its founder's originating point of view — convictions that are firmly grounded in the safeguarding mindset of quadrant C (Control).

An avid rock climber, founder Yvon Chouinard started out forging steel pitons, which he and fellow alpinists would hammer into cracks in the rock face, frequently causing damage. During an ascent on Yosemite's El Capitan in the early 1970s, Chouinard was deeply affected by the disfiguring impact of pitons. "I came home disgusted by the degradation I'd seen," he wrote in his memoir."[9] Chouinard soon became a leader in the "clean climbing" movement, shifting his business from steel pitons to aluminum chocks that can be wedged into cracks instead of hammered.

With this and other experiences, Chouinard fixed his conviction that humanity is ruining nature, that the environmental decline is a crisis, and that business can be part of the solution. That point of view is the fuel that feeds Patagonia's culture. Today, it's sustained through a variety of workplace policies:

- The company hires environmental activists.

- Employees can get paid to do a two-month externship at an environmental nonprofit of their choice.

- Guest speakers are regularly brought in to discuss environmental issues of the day.

- The best parking spaces are reserved for fuel-efficient vehicles, and any employee who chooses to go "driverless" (walking, biking, or skateboarding to work) gets a quarterly payout.

- The company's "Let My People Go Surfing" policy encourages workers to get away from their desks and experience nature daily — whether it's a midday bike ride or a spontaneous afternoon hike. The Ventura office includes a storage room for surfboards and a sign displaying the daily wave report.

- Job interviews often take place out in nature, sometimes while surfing.

These programs and policies produce a meaning-filled culture, and that culture leads the organization to perform at a high level. Within Patagonia, the individual brains all act in concert, and that cohesion maximizes the output of the company's energies.

In the field of neuropsychology, there's a popular expression (most often credited to Dr. Rick Hanson): the brain takes its shape from what the mind rests on. In the same way, you can shape your organization's culture by continually reinforcing your brand's unique point of view. In turn, a stronger, more cohesive culture will fuel your business progress. In their classic comparison study *Built to Last,* Jim Collins and Jerry Porras found, "The crucial variable is not the content of a company's ideology, but how deeply it believes its ideology and how consistently it lives, breathes, and expresses it in all that it does."[10]

Inside-Out Branding

Engaging and aligning your employees is one of the most effective ways to build your brand in market. That's because the biggest factor shaping the external identity of a brand is the internal identity of its providers.

Does that sound crazy? Try telling that to Patagonia. Describing the experience of a Patagonia customer, former VP of Marketing Joy Howard told *The Hub*, "It's not a brand experience that comes out of endless meetings debating what the brand experience should be. It's just a reflection of our values and the way we work."[11]

In fact, the DNA of an internal culture can have a surprising impact on the customer's experience, often through subtle cues that signal the provider's priorities. The producers of *CBS Sunday Morning* once staged a fascinating experiment related to this effect. They gave a top sommelier two different glasses of syrah, each made by a different French winery. The identity of the two vintners was concealed. One came from a traditional family winery with a long history of winemaking. The son who runs it studied oenology at university. The other syrah came from the Provençal version of a frat house, led by a fun-loving divorcé and his pals. Based on taste alone, the sommelier was asked to describe the type of personalities that produced each wine. He accurately described one vintner as "serious" and "precise" and the other as "friendly" and "spontaneous."[12]

This law of "inside-out identity" has been observed by leaders in both industry and culture. Zappos CEO Tony Hsieh says, "A company's culture and a company's brand are really just two sides of the same coin."[13] And Elvis Presley observed, "Values are like fingerprints. Nobody's are the same, but you leave 'em all over everything you do."

In other words, the foremost markers of your creed are the cues and codes that are embedded in your brand experience. Often unconsciously, customers interrogate your brand's behaviors, across all aspects of your enterprise, and they discern the brand's intentions by how the brand acts, not just by what it says. As Steve Jobs famously said, "People impute."

In their discernment of your brand, your customers have an ever-widening view into your company's inner workings. With the explosion of social media and mass access to information online, the membrane between the inner workings of your company and the external customer world is now permeable, magnifying the need for a coherent brand culture. The former Marketing VP at IBM, John Kennedy, described the situation at his company:

> We are living in a world where our customers have more visibility into us – the company behind the services and offerings. So we are driving a big change inside IBM, partnering with HR to look hard at the IBM brand as a reflection of our culture, the way we operate and our IBMers. So much of a brand is a reflection of its employees, and we are stepping in with our colleagues in the C-suite to understand how our culture should reflect that.[14]

In order to ensure that all your cues and codes are congruent with your creed, you need an aligned group of experience providers. From your website manager to your call center associates, every steward of every touchpoint must be fully imbued with your creed. As Bill Taylor, the cofounder of *Fast Company* magazine, asserted in the *Harvard Business Review,* "You can't be special, distinctive, and compelling in the marketplace unless you create something special, distinctive, and compelling in the workplace."[15]

Building a Brand Culture within a House of Brands

It's one thing to build a creed-inspired culture within a single-brand company. But what if you run an individual brand within a broader house of brands?

In that case, you can unleash the power of creed through "sub-culturing" — building a semi-autonomous "branded house" within the house of brands. For inspiration, you can look to the Aveda house within Estée-Lauder, the Ben & Jerry's house within Unilever, and the Zappos house within Amazon.

When I worked at Procter & Gamble, I witnessed a sub-culturing success firsthand: inside the set of cubicles that turned around Old Spice. The Old Spice brand is part of P&G's sizable beauty portfolio. Entering the new millennium, consumers saw Old Spice as being, well, old. There wasn't much spice. All that changed in 2010, when muscle-bound Isaiah Mustafa rode a horse through a Wieden+Kennedy-produced ad called "The Man Your Man Could Smell Like." That began a multi-year run that returned the venerable icon to the top of its category.

Behind that turnaround was a pop-up sub-culture. It started with the brand manager: a twenty-something "man's man" who seemed to be typecast for the job. Although James Moorhead and his small team were surrounded by brand groups dedicated to Olay and other mega-priorities, they created a little cubicle world of their own and, in a fun celebration of "mansmanship," adopted the symbols and spirit of college Greek life. They dubbed themselves "Omega Sigma," developed a pledge and associated insignia, and extended membership to their brethren at Wieden+Kennedy. Within this jocular-macho environment, the "Smell Like a Man" smash was born.

In order to build a creed-inspired culture, you must take a systematic approach to employee engagement. If you're not even in the ballpark today, it may represent a major organizational change initiative. As depicted in the model below, that agenda has three components: (1) initiating employees to the creed, (2) perpetuating commitment to the creed, and (3) demonstrating commitment to the creed from the top. With dedication to these priorities, you can sustainably align the values of your workforce and scale your organization's purposeful passion.

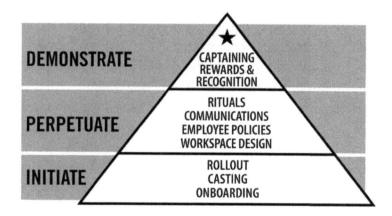

Initiating Employees to the Creed

Rollout

In your journey of organizational transformation, the initial launch to your employees is a critical priority — an incomparable moment to stir organizational conviction. Your goal is to make sure the language and meaning of your creed is clearly understood. But more significantly, it must be deeply *felt*. Your aim is for every member of your organization to develop a personal affinity for the content.

A formal launch event can take many forms — from an all-hands webcast to a cascading roadshow. Regardless of format, there are three keys to success: (1) active involvement by top management, (2) experiential internalization, and (3) a symbolic act that demonstrates authentic commitment.

The first critical feature is direct involvement by the top executive. In order to convey the critical nature of the content, he or she needs to be seen as leading it, and his or her personal conviction must be palpable. Passion is persuasive, and it ripples outward. Because of this phenomenon, the launch event represents a vital opportunity to trigger a "chain of conviction" — because the leader feels moved, your organization feels moved; and when your organization feels moved, it moves the world. In his or her remarks, the senior leader must make an authentic display of personal passion, relaying how the newly articulated creed relates to his or her individual life circumstance and priorities.

As an outcome of the launch, each of your employees must feel the same personal connection to the creed that the leader does. This requires an experiential component to the program — some form of engagement that gives your people an opportunity to internalize the creed at an individual level. What part of the employee's life story connects to the brand belief system and purpose? How do his or her personal values and priorities align with the creed? There are many ways to facilitate that reflection — from a guided collage-making exercise to a one-on-one interview.

When KPMG renewed its purpose in 2014, the company drove internalization through an app, built around the concept that "We Shape History" (*a supporting video by that title is publicly available on YouTube*). The theme was presented in posters that were displayed throughout KPMG's offices worldwide. Through a program and app called the "10,000 Stories

Challenge," the company then invited employees to design their own personal posters, mirroring the corporate ones. In the end, employees generated more than forty-thousand individual "story posters," and on the heels of the launch campaign, morale scores soared.[16]

In order for the launch to be seen as a true transformation in approach, your leadership team needs to put concrete policy changes behind the creed. Right out of the gate, your employees need to see that the enterprise is "walking the talk" — authentically living it before giving it to the world. Announcing a "symbolic act" can go a long way toward establishing credibility behind the creed. Whatever that act is, it must be demonstrative and declarative of the content of the creed.

My client Pharmavite nailed this part of the launch sequence. Grounded in the prime value of vitality, Pharmavite's purpose is to "bring the gift of health to life." During the company's cascading deployment, the leadership launched a series of initiatives that showed it was truly invested in its intention. Those employee initiatives included weekly deliveries of fresh fruit, free vitamins, and one-on-one coaching from registered dietitians.

The launch event is a one-of-kind opportunity to stir organizational conviction. By leveraging these three success factors — involvement by top management, experiential internalization, and a symbolic act — your deployment can effectively capture your employees' hearts and set the stage for an enduring transformation.

Cultivating Activation Agents

Of course, no leader can go it alone. Critically, he or she needs the full commitment of his or her executive team. If there's resistance among next-level leaders, the agenda will fail. For this reason, it's critical to enroll the top echelons of the hierarchy prior to engaging frontline employees. The "chain of conviction" can't have any broken links.

In order to sustain cultural captaincy, many organizations find value in appointing dedicated agents. Google staffs a "Chief Culture Officer" who leads a network of "culture clubs" across its seventy-plus offices.[17] LinkedIn has 250 "Culture Champions" who organize an average of 48 employee events each year.[18] And inside my client Pharmavite, there are "Vitali-teams" – comprised of multifunctional leaders at each location – who ensure that the company's prime value of vitality remains a hallmark of the culture.

Casting

Given the perpetual turnover every organization experiences, a one-time rollout isn't sufficient. On an ongoing basis, every new employee must be brought into the fold "on purpose." It starts with your employer branding efforts. Use your employer brand to "cast" for candidates who intrinsically hold your values. Feature your creed on your career website. Embed it in your job postings.

Putting your creed out there is a powerful way to attract talent. A 2011 report commissioned by the Career Advisory Board found that, among young adults aged 21 to 31, the top factor they want in a career is a sense of meaning.[19] More recently, a Korn Ferry survey of more than a thousand recruiters found that job candidates are making final employment decisions based on a company's culture and purpose rather than the actual benefits package.[20]

A related story comes from one of my clients: Beech-Nut, makers of all-natural baby food, whose purpose is to "inspire a lifelong joy of real food." In the fall of 2015, a supply chain leader attended a career fair at Clarkson University in upstate

New York, about 200 miles from the company's facilities. The fair featured a number of marquee employers like General Electric and Target, and it kicked off with a panel presentation. Each company representative shared a little bit about what his or her firm does, and Beech-Nut was the last to go. In his brief remarks, he boldly proclaimed that Beech-Nut is in the "joy" business, working every day to bring the joy of real food to parents and babies. The pronouncement hit the room like a thunderclap, and at the booth sessions that followed, he and his HR partner couldn't handle the disproportionate volume of job seekers.

To find the best, most creed-congruent candidates, consider adopting a screening activity that's unique to your values. Looking for a fun spark in its employees, Zappos asks candidates to name something weird that they've done. An interview at Virgin may involve singing or dancing. Seeking exuberance in the people it hires, Harrah's conducts an *American Idol*-style audition.[21]

To create a creed-aligned culture, there's no stronger lever than to hire like-minded employees. Some call the process "typecasting," and while that might sound a little monocratic, shared motivations are the hallmark of any winning team. It's less about a profile and more about a *mindset*. In the words of author Denise Lee Yohn, the goal is to "produce unity, not uniformity, within your workforce."[22]

This approach of hiring for "DNA not MBA," as authors Shaun Smith and Andy Milligan term it, was pioneered by Southwest Airlines over forty years ago and has been fully adopted by companies like Zappos, Warby Parker, and Virgin. From the employees' standpoint, this is what they want as well. More than 70 percent of Gen-Zers say it's critical to work somewhere that aligns with their individual values.[23]

Onboarding

Another way to initiate new employees to your creed is to actually "initiate" them. Starting a new job is a highly charged experience and the perfect opportunity for imprinting cultural priorities. There are two components to the initiation process: instruction and induction.

The first step involves teaching the foundational tenets – the convictions, values and purpose. Many leading institutions have a formal "college" program. Steve Jobs commissioned a dean from Yale to build Apple U., which uses case studies to instill the same kind of decision-making values that he applied. At Pirch, the company's "Ambassador of Joy" leads every employee through a five-day immersion that touches on all twenty-three of the company's "elements of joy."[24] And at USAA – the duty-bound provider of insurance to military families – new employees are told, "Get your affairs in order and report to the personnel processing facility." There, they eat the same MREs (meals ready to eat) that servicemen and women consume and read letters written by combat personnel in the field.[25] At the conclusion, they make a promise to provide extraordinary service to the military members who did the same for their country.[26]

A second step in the process is induction. The solemnity of a ceremonial installation helps to cement the commitment. Here are three examples:

- At Disney, you're not a "cast member" until you've completed the "Disney Traditions" course at Disney University. At the conclusion of the program, the conference room doors swing open, and Mickey Mouse arrives with a gift box. The box contains the iconic nametags that will be worn by the new employees, and Mickey himself confers them to the initiates.

- At Jack Daniels, new employees attend "Camp Jack." They travel to Lynchburg, Tennessee for several days of training, including one day working in the distillery. The final "induction ceremony" takes place on fabled Barbeque Hill, and each graduate is bestowed a nickname that links their identity to the Jack Daniel's legend.

- Gentle Giant is a five-star moving company based in Somerville, Massachusetts. In keeping with the company's value of hard work, a new mover doesn't become a true "Giant" until he or she has completed a rite of passage — a run up and down the steps of Harvard Stadium.

Perpetuating Commitment to the Creed

Rituals

One of the most powerful ways to perpetuate your organization's sense of purpose is to establish rituals. According to anthropologists, rituals are a central feature of the human experience, and sociologists view them as a powerful device for forging bonds and establishing shared priorities. Very simply, they are prescribed customs that members of a particular culture engage in together on a regular basis. The strongest rituals are not only habitual; they're *meaningful*. They reinforce core convictions and values. Sports teams, military organizations, religious groups, membership societies — all use rituals to reinforce their mutuality and their commitment to a shared point of view.

In the professional sports arena, one of the most noteworthy rituals is the "Haka" dance performed by the New Zealand national rugby team, The All Blacks. Prior to kickoff, the players perform a native dance — aggressive stomping, arm slaps, and shouting — that is a symbolic expression of challenge. For the team members, it asserts their cohesion as a unit, and it reminds both the players and their opponents of the team's deep heritage. It's a defining feature of the enterprise and the brand.

Major businesses use rituals as well. Since 1975, teams throughout Walmart start their day by repeating the "Walmart Cheer."[27] At Specialized Bicycles, the employees go out for a ride at noon each day. On August 28 each year, UPS reaffirms its century-old principles by celebrating Founders Day.

Not all rituals involve an event. Some are norms of behavior. Take for example the Hawaiian cultural artifacts that pervade Salesforce. As founder Marc Benioff built the company, he was inspired by the Hawaiian spirit of 'ohana, reflecting a commitment to family and the supportive bonds that exist between its members. As enduring symbols of that beacon, many employees wear a Hawaiian shirt on Fridays and write "Aloha" in their email greetings.[28]

Often, business rituals include some element of employee recognition. By celebrating a particular employee (or employees), the leadership is able to show what the brand's creed looks like in practice. Here are two examples:

- At every Ritz-Carlton office and hotel around the world, employees start their day with a 15- to 20-minute "lineup" ritual. The members of each individual workgroup — a team of chefs in a kitchen, top executives in a boardroom, housekeeping staff near a supply room — gather in a circle with copies of the company's "Credo Card" on hand. The standard agenda involves reaffirming the Credo, reading aloud a guest letter and discussing how the core values impacted that guest's experience and the daily work they do. On Mondays and Fridays, the lineup agenda includes a story of an employee who demonstrated exceptional service.[29]

- Every Monday morning, all the employees of Innocent Drinks gather in the lobby of their West London head-quarters. One reason for the gathering is a quirky ritual called "the Lords and Ladies of the Sash." During the light-hearted ceremony, company leaders call out an employee to recognize his or her actions in support of the company creed. He or she dons the ceremonial sash along with a top hat or tiara, and everyone bows.

The Monday morning "all-hands huddle" is a particularly effective lever for perpetuating a brand's culture and creed, so much so that many other organizations — like Method, Plum Organics and Change.org — have adopted it. As part of Method's execution, the leaders hand out "values awards." Team members nominate someone by submitting a short story, and during the huddle, the winners spin a wheel to collect a prize. Cofounders Eric Ryan and Adam Lowry say, "At Method, the huddle is our way of aligning our obsessions with our objec-tives and keeping the company on track." They add, "The value of the huddle is in reminding all that their individual contri-bution fits within the larger ecosystem."[30]

Communications

Just as we all need iPhone reminders to help us keep track of our priorities, the members of your organization need con-tinual nudges and avowals of the creed. They need reinforcing messages in order to sustain the motivation and their sense of identity and direction.

It starts with the leader. To perpetuate commitment to the creed, the top leader must continually "talk the talk." Describing the vital priorities of a CEO, Merck chairman Ken Frazier says, "Number one is that sense of purpose and direction that the company needs, making sure that that's always clear and people know what we're all about."[31]

In fulfilling that role, it's almost impossible for leadership to over-communicate. According to a study by Tenet Partners, only one in five employees strongly agree that their company leadership communicates how their brand's values should be lived.[32] In that regard, the leadership should use every opportunity to reassert parts of the creed: in town halls, in one-on-one settings, at the start of team meetings, etc. At one of my clients (a major pharmaceutical company), a senior leader signs off all her emails to employees by thanking the person for his or her help in fulfilling the franchise purpose.

Another critical enabler is corporate communications. All the standard internal communications vehicles apply: the company intranet, employee manuals, enterprise newsletters, badges, screensavers, etc. Other devices for purposeful "invertising" include a pocket credo card and a desktop display item. Your company events are another opportunity to give visibility to purpose and convictions.

Telling Stories

Because humans are wired for story, it's one of the most powerful methods for communicating purpose and convictions. Neuroscience shows that a good narrative stimulates attention and embeds the message in people's memories. As such, it's an effective way to impart your creed and inspire and direct action.

A story is simply a recounting of an event, and it typically has an arc with three parts: (1) a beginning — setting up the context, (2) a middle action sequence, and (3) an outcome. The most evocative stories involve a tension or conflict: the hero overcomes an obstacle. This is an opportunity to reinforce a "moral" that celebrates the creed.

One of the most motivating stories you can tell is your heritage story. It reminds your employees of the larger arc that they're a part of. It puts a spotlight on the customer need that was the genesis for the business, and it provides a memorable and meaningful context for present-day work.

At other times, the content for stories will come from your customers or employees. At Motorola Solutions, employees are encouraged to submit stories of specific moments when a customer took heroic action utilizing a Motorola product. The company then shares those stories via a continuous video loop on closed circuit TVs.

Employee Policies

If you pull up to Harley-Davidson's headquarters in a car, you won't feel very welcome. Signs posted on the front brick wall declare, "No cages. Motorcycles only." To find parking, you'll have to take your constraining vehicle elsewhere.

Workplace perks and policies help to reinforce an organization's point of view, and frequently, the impact of the creed starts in the parking lot. At Patagonia, the best spaces are reserved for fuel-efficient vehicles. At Pampers, expectant moms get the plum spots.

There's plenty you can do inside the building as well, by putting your money where your creed is. Egalitarian-minded IKEA gives all its part-time workers full benefits; and to perpetuate Whole Foods' team-focused culture, the company capped executives' salaries at no more than 19 times the income of an average worker.

You can also use employee policies to encourage your people to get out and live the lifestyle that your creed espouses. Airbnb employees get a quarterly travel credit to use at any Airbnb listing. And when SunTrust Bank set out to "light the way to financial well-being" for its customers, it first did so for its employees. It granted an extra day off so employees could get their personal finances in order, and it offered a variety of internal resources to help.

Workspace Design

Winston Churchill once declared, "There is no doubt whatever about the influence of architecture and structure upon human character and action. We make our buildings and afterwards they make us. They regulate the course of our lives."

The psychological effects that Churchill asserted are difficult to prove, but we do know that environmental factors can impact human behavior. Walls that are painted light blue are more calming. High ceilings encourage abstract thinking.[33]

In order to cultivate your desired employee experience, consider bringing your point of view to life in your physical workplace. Use environmental codes to support the narrative of your creed. Employ tangible signals that bring meaning to the physical setting.

Throughout the corporate life of Apple, its leadership has used environmental features to support the culture. In the early years, developers flew a pirate flag above the offices to symbolize the company's maverick intent. Later, Steve Jobs placed a Bosendorfer piano and a BMW motorcycle in the atrium to inspire topnotch craftsmanship. Within the marketing department, the words "Simplify, Simplify, Simplify" were painted on the walls. (For emphasis, the first two words had a strike-mark through them.) One of Steve's final legacies was the $5 billion "spaceship" building that landed in Cupertino in 2017.

As the Apple example illustrates, there is a range of ways in which environment can reinforce a point of view. One of the most basic tactics is to put the creed itself on display. At jetBlue, a montage of core values words decorates common spaces. In the offices of Weiden+Kennedy, a large piece of artwork made with pushpins proclaims the company's operating mantra: "Fail Harder." In the lobby of Johnson & Johnson's headquarters, the company's 300-word "Credo" is engraved in limestone. Posting the words in this way gives permanence to the ideas and emphasizes their primacy.

Following its split from Motorola Mobility in 2011, telecom equipment maker Motorola Solutions made an effective cultural intervention using workspace signage. To deploy its new purpose – "helping people be their best in moments that matter" – the leadership executed a surprise makeover of its thirty-seven facilities, simultaneously redecorating them over a single weekend. Walls were covered with larger-than-life images of customer heroes in "moments that matter," like a dispatcher calling for backup.

Another way to authenticate a point of view is through the use of meaningful totems. At Burt's Bees headquarters in Durham, North Carolina, the company has enshrined the converted turkey coop that founder Burt Shavitz once used as his home, relocating it from the Maine woods where he'd enjoyed a simple, back-to-nature lifestyle.

At the most sophisticated level, you can use your physical environment to immerse your employees in the world of your point of view. Inside LEGO, playful workspaces are intentionally designed "to nurture the inner child." ING Group's open-air headquarters give physical form to its values of openness and transparency. Outside the walls of Natura – a Brazilian cosmetics company that honors biodiversity – a eucalyptus forest surrounds the building. Within IDEO's open floor plan, employees are encouraged to be creatively expressive in the way they decorate their cubicle space. Harley-Davidson's offices are a shrine to biker culture. The physical environment can even extend to the food choices that are available. In Airbnb's café, there's an ever-changing mix of options inspired by different travel destinations.[34]

Here are three more snapshots of immersive environments that cultivate a creed-fueled culture:

- Nike's Beaverton, Oregon campus contains a 400-meter running track, state-of-the-art gyms, two soccer fields, an Olympic-sized pool, a basketball court, and a putting green. The buildings are named for iconic athletes, and metal plaques profile stories of greatness. Inside the offices, there are display cases featuring the equipment of famous athletes, and TVs in the cafeterias broadcast sporting events.

- Returning to Innocent, the playful, "be natural" culture makes its home in a building dubbed the Fruit Towers (a nod to the John Cleese series *Fawlty Towers*). The central lounge area contains picnic tables, a Ping-Pong table, and large, inflatable bananas. The floor is covered in AstroTurf. Lighthearted images and sayings fill the walls, and a special corner of the building showcases the photos of everyone who's been recognized as a Lord or Lady of the Sash.

- Throughout the campus of Activision Blizzard, statues of game characters tower beside the entrances to buildings. Inside one lobby, a replica of a sword-wielding archangel is suspended fourteen feet above the floor. Work areas have names like "the Sanctuary," and throughout the facilities, shelves display ceremonial battle masks and shields.[35]

Demonstrating Commitment to the Creed

Captaining

All your efforts to initiate employees and perpetuate commitment to the creed will fail if your organization's leader isn't a visible advocate. There's truth in the adage that culture starts at the top. As the employee engagement model depicts, strong executive leadership creates the beacon.

As we've seen in next-gen leaders like Paul Polman, Tim Cook and Anita Roddick, the captains of creed-inspired entities are equal parts operator and "spiritual chieftain." While not every leader will have the innate pastoral skills of a Richard Branson or Howard Schultz, every creed-inspired boss must strive to emulate the type of captaincy they represent. As Anthony Tjan, CEO of venture capital firm Cue Ball, wrote in *Harvard Business Review,* "They must be the strongest representations of the firm's culture and purpose, not just writing or memorizing the mission statement, but rather internalizing and exemplifying what the company stands for."[36]

An exemplar is T-Mobile's John Legere. When he took the reins of the wireless carrier in 2012, he introduced a new "Uncarrier" creed — making it the firm's business to break the category's conventions. Marked by its brash magenta color and disruptive promotions, the brand quickly became a symbol of status-quo busting.

Concurrent with the launch of the "Uncarrier" creed, John shaped his personal image to match. Shedding the staid persona he exhibited in his early career, he adopted an un-CEO look by growing his hair long. He always wore magenta, and breaking standard executive protocols, he regularly dropped profanity-laden tweets that trolled his competitors. In 2014, he made news when he crashed an AT&T customer event.

Leadership guru John Maxwell defines a leader as someone who "knows the way, goes the way and shows the way."[37] That formula is particularly germane for creed-inspired organizations, which often refer to their convictions and purpose as "the way" (the Barclay's Way, the Starbucks Way, the Southwest Way, etc.).

As Maxwell prescribes, the first responsibility of a captain is to deeply "know" – and feel – the creed. If you are the leader, that starts with participating in the discovery of the enterprise convictions and values. But beyond that – or if you're new to the enterprise – you must seek out immersive experiences that inform and inspire your commitment to the cause. Ultimately, you need to establish the basis for your "moral authority" – one that entitles you to lead the movement and genuinely stirs the passion in others. It's not too much to say that a conviction-fired brand radiates from the heart of its leader.

One way to establish that influence and authority is through personal values sync. How do your personal values align to the company values? In your personal life, how have you experienced the "wrong" that the brand wants to right? How does the purpose connect to your sense of personal purpose and priorities?

Another way to establish "moral authority" is through a deep heritage immersion. Before taking the helm at Unilever, CEO Paul Polman spent hours and hours in the company archive studying Lord William Lever. As an outside hire, he made it his business to know the founder's personal philosophy better than most anyone else.[38]

Lastly, you as a leader, along with your fellow top leaders, can gain inspiration and clout through regular "moccasins missions." By walking a mile in your customers' shoes, you can garner intimate insight into the motivations that fuel your enterprise. In the case of Harley-Davidson, it's not a walk but a ride. Former CMO Mark-Hans Richer said of his company, "It's a leadership trait to be out riding with our customers. If you're not out riding and being out at rallies and hitting the road with customers, you're kind of not seen as living up to the company's ideals. Engaging with customers is a big part of what we believe is very important. And that helps you get at understanding those ideals and also reinforcing those ideals through firsthand, day-to-day customer contact."[39]

In organizations that are truly creed-inspired, "showing the way" means that the leader personifies the values and convictions. The leader animates and authenticates the enterprise point of view through personal image and actions: how he or she looks and spends his or her time. As Albert Schweitzer once observed, "Example is not the main thing in influencing others. It is the only thing."[40] Here are some examples:

- Around the halls of IKEA, where humbleness and cost-consciousness reign, the late founder Ingvar Kamprad used to wear secondhand clothes, and he reused tea bags.[41]

- The leaders of Meguiar's (makers of high-end car care products) are car aficionados, and they frequent car shows, always wearing the stylish, all-black uniforms that are a code of the brand.

- At accounting and consulting firm Crowe Horwath, CEO Jim Powers lives out the company's value of fun by staging April Fools' Day pranks and by wearing historical period costumes when making grand announcements about the company.[42]

Lastly, Maxwell's "going the way" means that you the leader need to "walk the walk." In order for your employees to be fully engaged in your creed, they must see the leadership taking actions based on the creed: setting strategy and allocating resources on purpose, partnering with suppliers who share your convictions, and aligning enterprise activities to support your creed. Decisions and programs should be linked to the creed. It should be a daily discussion among managers.

Unfortunately, there are big gaps in this area. According to research by PricewaterhouseCoopers, only 34 percent of business leaders report using purpose as a guidepost for decision-making. Only 27 percent make efforts to explicitly connect purpose to individuals' work.[43]

One of the most powerful signals of a creed is leadership's response in difficult situations. As the saying goes, true values are shown when adherence has a cost. When I was starting out in my P&G career, then-CEO John Pepper affirmed the company's value of integrity in the way he responded to a 2001 "dumpster diving" incident. When he learned that contractors for P&G had taken documents from the trash outside a competitor's offices, John quarantined the material, notified the company and, although the actions didn't violate any laws, made a $10 million payment to the firm for damages.[44] Actions like that one provide powerful confirmation of the governing creed.

Rewards and Recognition

Another way to demonstrate conviction for the creed is for you the leader to recognize and reward employees for behaviors that are consistent with the purpose and convictions. Using the example of fellow employees is an effective way to guide others' behavior. Repeating the contention of Albert Schweitzer, "Example is not the main thing in influencing others. It is the only thing."

Here, KIND founder and CEO Daniel Lubetzky describes a monthly recognition program that supports the brand's ideal of kindness:

> At KIND, one way we show each other we care is through our KINDOs program — our version of 'kudos.' Each month, team members celebrate a colleague for doing things the KIND Way. Sometimes these recognitions are performance-based, but more often, they recount how someone approached a conversation or handled a situation with kindness and respect.[45]

Another example is REI's annual "Anderson Awards," named for the company's founders. It is a peer-based recognition program that acknowledges employees "who exemplify REI core values while positively impacting the business in ways that further REI's purpose and strategies."

In all your incentive efforts, ensure there's alignment with your purpose and values. Establish KPIs — and supporting bonus structures — that support your creed. For example, at Zappos, where happiness reigns, call center employees are measured on consumer satisfaction rather than call length (the industry standard). Only when people's incentives point them toward the creed will those ideals govern their daily behaviors.

Case for Action

- The most significant opportunity of purpose is employee engagement. Purpose motivates the workforce and inspires excellence and creativity.
- The more deeply and broadly an organization holds a common belief system, the more likely it is that the enterprise will function at a high level.
- Engaging and aligning your employees is one of the most effective ways to build your brand in market. That's because the biggest factor shaping the external identity of a brand is the internal identity of its providers.

Actions to Take

- Initiate your employees to your creed with an inspiring rollout. Key success factors include: active involvement by top management, experiential internalization, and a symbolic act that demonstrates authentic commitment.
- Bring new employees onboard "on purpose." Cast for candidates who intrinsically hold your convictions, and consummate their commitment to the creed through a robust onboarding process and a formal induction.
- Perpetuate commitment to the creed using rituals, communications, employee policies, and workspace design.
- Demonstrate commitment as a leader. Establish "moral authority" by seeking out immersive experiences that inform and inspire your devotion to the creed. "Show the way" by personifying the point of view, and "go the way" by walking the talk. A key way to reinforce employee commitment is through a program of rewards and recognition.

CHAPTER 4
Develop Offerings with Intent

The creation of a thousand forests is in one acorn.
—Ralph Waldo Emerson, Essays and Poems

Fuel for Perpetual Value Creation

Ultimately, adopting a creed-inspired approach to your business is about value creation. Here's how the co-founder of HP, David Packard, described it back in 1960:

I want to discuss *why* a company exists in the first place. In other words, why are we here? I think many people assume, wrongly, that a company exists simply to make money. While this is an important result of a company's existence, we have to go deeper and find the real reasons for our being. As we investigate this, we inevitably come to the conclusion that a group of people get together and exist as an institution that we call a company so they are able to accomplish something collectively that they could not accomplish separately — they make a contribution to society, a phrase which sounds trite but is fundamental . . . [In the broader world] you can look around and still see people who are interested in money and nothing else, but the underlying drives come largely from a desire to do something else — to make a product — to give a service — generally to do something which is of value.[1]

That's the power and promise of purpose. It puts the business in service of people and the world. It directs the organization to fulfill human needs and aspirations. Profits are the outcome.

In this mode, an enterprise is simultaneously focused and unleashed — focused on addressing a particular need state and unleashed from the constraints of specific business parameters. Take the example of The North Face:

Named for the challenging side of a mountain, The North Face exists to inspire and equip a global movement of exploration. In that quest, it continually expands and upgrades its outdoor technologies. "We push the boundaries of innovation so that you can push the boundaries of exploration," the brand's website says.

After first developing extreme skiwear in the 1980s, the brand soon added its Tekware™ collection for rock climbers and backpackers. Other exploration-inspired offerings have included a heat-generating jacket and a vest with a built-in airbag to help skiers and trekkers in the event of an avalanche. The brand has also invented new fibers like its ThermoBall™ insulation and a new rubber compound for higher-performance trail shoes.

This kind of perpetual innovation is not uncommon for a purpose-driven enterprise. The call to "serve" unleashes a never-ending cycle of new value creation. In comparing different types of organizations, a 2014 study by Deloitte found that purpose-driven enterprises are two times more likely to invest in new technologies.[2]

Uniquely Purposeful Offerings

Innovation can arise from any number of places: the identification of unmet needs, research on base technologies, the habits and practices of extreme users, etc. Within a creed-inspired organization, a unique lens for innovating is the purpose itself. A great illustration is the revival of the Barbie brand:

Prior to the middle of this decade, the Barbie brand was a bit tarnished, and throughout 2012 and 2013, sales fell every quarter. But with a wave of female empowerment sweeping the culture, the original "girl possibilities" brand was well positioned for a comeback.

Barbie began its resurgence by renewing its commitment to "inspire and nurture the limitless possibilities of girls," which was the original purpose that motivated Barbie's founder. One manifestation of the renewed purpose is the brand's "Sheroes" line – dolls that are designed in the likeness of real-life inspirations. Two of the first figures to be introduced were Olympic gymnast Gabby Douglas and director Ana Duvernay. Later, in celebration of International Women's Day 2018, the brand unveiled seventeen new likenesses, including those of aviation pioneer Amelia Earhart and British Olympic boxer Nicola Adam. The inclusion of counterintuitive body types — like that of plus-size model Ashley Graham — earned the brand a wealth of social media support.

The revamped product lineup was supported by a campaign called "Imagine the Possibilities." In one execution, a little girl gave a lecture in front of a real college class. The campaign hit the mainstream with a targeted buy during the Thanksgiving Day 2015 parade, and on a tide of attentive eyeballs and positive sentiment, the brand returned to growth.

Another beacon of purposeful innovation is Oprah Winfrey. In polls, she ranks as the most admired entrepreneur. And no wonder. Born into poverty, she is now the richest self-made woman in America, with a net worth of $3 billion dollars, and her 35-year-old media brand is one of the strongest in the world. Of her sense of purpose, Oprah says it formed when she was a young girl. Despite the inherent limits she faced in small-town Mississippi, she had big dreams for her life. "I wanted to be a teacher. And to be known for inspiring my students to be more than they thought they could be. I never imagined it would be on TV," she writes.[3]

That sense of purpose was her guide as she hosted the smash *Oprah Winfrey Show* for 25 years. In the 1990s, as other talk shows grabbed ratings with tabloid content, Oprah remained true to her "live your best life" focus. Today, she manifests her purpose through her *O Magazine* (circulation: 2.4 million) and Oprah.com, which receives 13 million users each month generating 75 million page views.[4] In another leap of purposeful innovation, she created OWN: The Oprah Winfrey Network in a joint venture with Discovery Communications. Despite some early ratings struggles, OWN has grown to become the most-watched network among African-American women. Speaking about her philosophy with regard to programming, Oprah told a Stanford University audience:

> I don't do anything without being fully clear about why I intend to do it . . . So I say to my producers, "Come to me with your intention – whatever it is, whatever shows you're proposing, whatever ideas you're proposing – and then I will decide based on the intention." Do I really want to do this? Is this how we really want to use this platform? That really is the secret to why we were number one all those years. It was because it was intention-fueled, intention-based, coming out of purposeful programming.[5]

As the examples of Barbie and Oprah highlight, the lens of purpose can lead to the development of unique, one-of-a-kind offerings. And these purposeful product platforms can be the source of breakout business success. To that point, research by global banking giant HSBC concluded that Millennial entrepreneurs are achieving greater success than older generations because they are motivated by purpose over profit.[6]

Creating Value Across Platforms

In the case of Oprah, purpose has led her to grow her business across platforms. The same is true for Disney. In its quest to bring happiness to millions, the company has migrated from movies and theme parks to cruises and streaming services.

CVS is on a similar journey. In his efforts to help people on their path to better health, CEO Larry Merlo is systemically remaking the drugstore chain into a champion and catalyst for health. The company is aggressively building its network of walk-in clinics, and its acquisition of insurer Aetna promises to create a major disruption in the way Americans receive their healthcare.

With a prime value and purpose, a brand gains greater elasticity to grow across platforms. There are wide-open lanes for value creation, broad space to stretch into new adjacencies. By contrast, defining your business in product terms can put it in a box, where it can become squeezed into obsolescence. The textbook cases are Kodak and Toys "R" Us.

Under Armour's founder and CEO Kevin Plank has hooked his company's expansion to the ideal of performance. In a speech at South by Southwest, he declared, "I do like being defined as a 'performance company.' I think it's completely unlimiting. It's an untethered approach to the way that we see the ability to define our company."[7] Untethered from its sportswear roots, Under Armour has an ever-expanding digital portfolio. Following its acquisitions of MapMyFitness, EndoMondo, and MyFitnessPal, the company is now the largest digital health and fitness company in the world.[8]

Another case of purposeful stretch is Mars Petcare. Serving almost half of the world's population of dogs and cats, Mars' Petcare business leads with a point of view and purpose: "We believe that pets make the world better for us, so we make it our purpose to make a better world for pets."[9] As the maker of Iams, Royal Canin and Pedigree, the core of Mars' business is pet food; but its purpose has led it to innovate into services. The franchise now owns the four largest pet hospital chains, making it the largest employer of vets in North America. Today two-thirds of Mars Petcare's employees work in services. Through a new pet-fitness subsidiary, the group is now using connected devices to generate breakthroughs in preventative pet health.

Perhaps the most celebrated omni-platform success is Red Bull. In the words of founder and CEO Dietrich Mateschitz, "Red

Bull isn't a drink, it's a way of life."[10] As a symbol of daring, it sits firmly in quadrant A (Achieve), and it's built on the conviction that limits are to be challenged. That philosophy is on display in its video of a 12-year-old skateboarder completing three revolutions off a ramp jump and in the broadcast of Felix Baumgartner skydiving from the edge of space.

Of course, Red Bull has sold an ocean of drinks — 68 billion cans worth since the company was founded[11] — but on the wings of a compelling creed, it sells a whole lot more. The company's businesses include sports teams, stadiums, a record label, and a magazine. It produces events, music, and films.

Red Bull's thrill-seeking point of view springs from its virile founder. Not surprisingly, Mateschitz is a Taurus, and his passions include flying, snowboarding, and motocross. The unshaven, open-shirted 74-year-old has never married, calling himself "too immature."[12]

The outside identity of Red Bull is fueled by an internal culture that's youthfully high-octane. The company plucks new recruits off college campuses and screens them for fully charged energy levels. The headquarters building in Austria is shaped like a volcano and features a dominant piece of bronze sculpture: a herd of large bulls bursting out of the atrium and into a lake. Regional offices look like high-end nightclubs, featuring skateboard ramps and slides.

Guided by a subsidiary called Red Bull Media House, the company is a content provider as well as a beverage producer. It adds value to young people's lives not just by delivering energy to their bloodstream, but also by quenching their thirst for adrenaline. Consumers can get amped by consuming a beverage, by perusing breathtaking photography in *The Red Bulletin,* by attending a Crashed Ice event, or by watching an adventure series on Red Bull TV.

Oprah, Under Armour, Mars Petcare, and Red Bull — all are

examples of brands that have grown across platforms on the wings of a prime value and purpose. To get there with your business, think of your brand not only as a value proposition but also as a *values* proposition. Think not only in terms of products and physical value but also services and "metaphysical" value. Ask yourself:

- Beyond our base category, where does our prime value lead us?
- Ignoring category norms, what does our purpose compel us to do?
- In what ways can we more fully manifest our desired reality for the world?

Intentional Experience Design

In the quest to serve and add value, there's a breakthrough approach that too many companies have been slow to adopt. It comes from research by Alan Zorfas and Daniel Leemon, representing the insights firms Motista and CEB. Their findings were published in the *Harvard Business Review* in August 2016.

In their work, Zorfas and Leemon examined hundreds of brands in dozens of categories, looking at how they create customer value. What they found is that the Holy Grail for profitable outcomes is not the usual target of "customer satisfaction." Instead, the most effective way to maximize customer value is to fulfill an "emo-motivation" — ideals like belonging and freedom. The outcome of that focus is more emotionally connected customers. "On a lifetime value basis, emotionally connected customers are more than twice as valuable as highly satisfied customers," they found.[13]

In my language, an "emo-motivation" is the prime value discussed in Chapter 2 — the motivation at the center of your purpose. By making that the focus of your product experience, you will achieve better financial outcomes than you will by pursuing customer satisfaction for its own sake. Affirming that approach, Sir Richard Branson writes, "I'm convinced that it is feelings — and feelings alone — that account for the success of the Virgin brand in all its myriad forms."[14]

Consistent with the findings of Zorfas and Leemon, the strongest brands create a product (or service) experience that "bleeds a creed." For luxury beauty brand Aesop, the prime value is wisdom. Its bookish offerings are thoughtfully curated in a monastic spa. By contrast, Aesop's competitor Lush emphasizes genuineness and displays its products in all their naked glory in an environment that feels like a farm stand. Both brands deliver skin and body care benefits, produce highly satisfied customers, and generate strong emotional connections, but the motivation governing each experience is completely different.

Here are three examples of service experiences that were intentionally designed to fulfill a prime value:

- The golden child of the fast-food industry, Chick-fil-A runs on the Golden Rule. The company's purpose is to "glorify God by being a faithful steward of all that is entrusted to us, and to have a positive influence on all who come in contact with Chick-fil-A." Through its in-store operations, the company aims to deliver an experience of grace. That starts with in-depth employee training, emphasizing that every life has a story that deserves empathy. With that awareness, service providers strive to offer what CEO Dan Cathy calls "amenities and kindness that minister to the heart."[15] Their efforts include a commitment to "Second Mile Service." Referencing a Biblical passage, it calls for every employee to go above and beyond in his or her ministry to customers. That may include ushering a customer to his car holding an umbrella or carrying a tray for a mother with young children. These small pleasantries — congruent expressions of creed — have earned the brand a legion of hardcore fans. In recent years, the company has grown at about 13 percent annually,[16] and even though it remains closed for business on Sundays, it still manages to sell three times as much as competitors like KFC."[17]

- Development Bank of Singapore (DBS Bank) is the largest bank in Southeast Asia, and its purpose is to "make banking joyful." One of the biggest pain points for banking customers is wait times, and eight years ago, many customers said that DBS stood for "damn bloody slow." The company began its journey toward joy by working on each individual "process event," eventually taking 250 million hours of customer wait time out of its system.[18] With joy as its design objective — and joy KPIs in its corporate scorecard — the company also remodeled its branches, using new technology to create a more joyful customer experience. One joy-inducing initiative was the addition of portable ATMs at branches during the busy Chinese New Year season in order to alleviate wait times.[19] CEO Piyush Gupta told *Forbes*, "Almost three-fourths of the world would rather go to the dentist than to a bank. If DBS is successful in making it less of a painful chore, then we think we can create a very different kind of bank, one that is a joy to bank with."[20] So far, the results of its efforts have been upbeat. During 2017 and 2018, the bank experienced sustained momentum in total income and profit.[21]

- Having notched 45 consecutive years of profitability, Southwest Airlines is the envy of the airline industry.

One of the key drivers of that success is the strength of its brand experience — one that conveys a consistent feeling of warm-heartedness. The brand's imagery includes a heart logo. Signs on its baggage carts read, "Cart with a heart," and the pretzel bags say, "Just because we like you." Policies like no baggage fees, no change fees, and free inflight TV feel generous and benevolent, and the airline's staff is famously relatable and fun-loving. The five-dollar happy hours they offer contribute to an overall experience that feels more like a backyard BBQ than a typical cattle haul.

All three of these brands inherently follow the guidance of famed Indian monk Swami Vivekananada, who said, "Take up one idea. Make that one idea your life — think of it, dream of it, live on that idea. Let the brain, muscles, nerves, every part of your body, be full of that idea, and just leave every other idea alone. This is the way to success."

Case for Action

- A creed is fuel for perpetual value creation. It puts your business in service of people and the world. It directs your organization to fulfill human needs and aspirations.

- The call to "serve" unleashes a never-ending cycle of new value creation.

- Using the lens of purpose to identify innovations often leads to the development of unique, one-of-a-kind offerings.

- Having a prime value gives your brand greater elasticity to grow across platforms.

- The most effective way to maximize customer value is to design your brand experience around your prime value.

Actions to Take

- Use the lens of purpose to innovate offerings that set your brand apart.

- Use your prime value as the conduit to grow across platforms. Think of your brand not only as a value proposition but also as a *values* proposition.

- Maximize customer value by making your brand's prime value the object of your product or service experience.

CHAPTER 5
Display Social Commitment

"Business!" cried the Ghost, wringing its hands
again. "Mankind was my business."
—Charles Dickens, A Christmas Carol

The Demand for Social Responsibility

In 1970, famed economist Milton Friedman argued, "The social responsibility of business is to increase its profits." Fifty years later, that's still true, but there's been a change in context.

Today, your business will most effectively maximize profits if it makes a social contribution. Being a good citizen helps you deliver a stronger bottom line.

What's driving this change is a generational shift in consumer expectations. Today's consumers demand that your brand demonstrate socially responsible behavior. That's because they're looking for fixes to the world's troubles, and globally, 53 percent of people believe brands can be more effective than governments.[1] Among U.S. consumers, 84 percent expect businesses to spur social change.[2]

Meanwhile, top talent wants to work for socially responsible brands. In fact, 51 percent of candidates won't work for a company that doesn't have strong social and environmental commitments.[3]

In general — across all of your brand's stakeholders — the "conscious capitalism" movement continues to gather steam. There's an accelerating push for brands to demonstrate sustainability and create "shared value" — win-wins for both business and society. Responding to these demands, there are now twenty-five hundred "B Corps" in the world — "public benefit corporations" that are certified to meet high standards of social and environmental performance.

If there were any business leaders still on the sidelines of the conscious capitalism movement, a heavyweight used a letter to push them onto the field. On January 16, 2018, the CEO of BlackRock, the world's largest asset manager, sent this message to the recipients of its $6 trillion in investments: if you want our funds, make a positive contribution to society. In his letter to fellow CEOs, Larry Fink wrote, "Society is demanding that companies, both public and private, serve a social purpose. To prosper over time, every company must not only deliver financial performance, but also show how it makes a positive contribution to society."[4]

A few months later, BlackRock used its financial weight to help stem the gun violence in America. Following the mass shooting at Stoneman Douglas High School in Parkland, Florida, the company pressed the gun manufacturers and retailers in its portfolio to tightly monitor who's buying firearms. Simultaneously, it created two new fund options that didn't include gun makers.

For your brand, a primary benefit of social responsibility is goodwill. Goodwill is a business asset — both an intangible asset on balance sheets and an operational asset as well. A virtuous reputation can help you forge partnerships and lure investors, and in the event of a crisis, it can help you weather the storm. As already implied, goodwill can also help you:

- *Land job candidates* — Today's MBA graduates would sacrifice an average of $13,700 in salary to work for a company that has a reputation for operating responsibly.[5]

- *Motivate employees* — Eighty-nine percent of employees want to be active in shaping their companies' responsible business practices.[6]

- *Attract consumers* — Eighty-five percent of consumers prefer brands that behave responsibly.[7]

Demonstrating Commitment through Actions

On February 5, 2014, CVS made one of the boldest pronouncements in the history of business: the company would stop selling tobacco products. Cigarettes — a front-of-store mainstay of pharmacies everywhere — would no longer be part of its brand proposition. Under the campaign banner of "CVS Quits for Good," CEO Larry Merlo announced, "Ending the sale of cigarettes and tobacco products at CVS Pharmacy is simply the right thing to do for the good of our customers and our company. The sale of tobacco products is inconsistent with our purpose — helping people on their path to better health."[8]

What made the move astounding was the financial sacrifice that it implied. Cigarettes are a destination category — they draw customers into drug stores — and with its decision, CVS would take a $2 billion, self-inflicted hit to its topline. Putting creed ahead of greed, Merlo asserted, "Tobacco products have no place in a setting where healthcare is delivered."[9]

Whatever CVS lost in sales, it immediately gained in goodwill. Merlo was lauded for his bravery, and nearly every corner of society applauded the company's integrity and responsibility in confronting a public health issue. Even President Barack Obama weighed in, with an official statement from the White House saying, "I congratulate — and thank — the CEO of CVS Caremark, Larry Merlo, the board of directors, and all who helped make a choice that will have a profoundly positive impact on the health of our country."[10]

What your brand does with its operations tells the world a lot about where you stand, particularly when adherence to your creed has a cost. Repeating an idea from the last chapter, values are transmitted by tradeoffs. And when your enterprise demonstrates courage of creed through its operational practices, it earns the esteem of your stakeholders. They are compelled by the feelings of congruence and commitment.

There are four ways to operationalize a commitment to social responsibility. They are: (1) your product's "provenance," (2) demonstrative policies, (3) branded cause programs, and (4) purposeful philanthropy.

Product Provenance

These days, a brand creates value not only through the benefits it provides but also in the way it delivers those benefits.

I call this "product provenance": its origins all along the supply chain. This includes the location of production, the source
materials, and the methods employed.

A central component of the sustainability agenda involves
"greening" your product's provenance. A benchmark in this
area is Method cleaning products. Method advocates for well-
being – the happiness and health of a "cleaner clean" – and
as a certified B Corp, the company endeavors to make clean-
ers that are good "for every surface, especially Earth's." (The
brand's manifesto appears in Appendix D.) The firm made a
major statement about its creed when it opened its first com-
pany-owned manufacturing facility in 2015; prior to that, the
company's products were produced and distributed by contractors. Forgoing cheaper "green field" options, it sited the facility
in Chicago's South Side, where its presence could help revitalize
a decaying neighborhood. Instead of cordoning off the site with
a fence, the property has open sidewalks leading to public green
space, and on the rooftop of the factory, a 75,000 square-foot
garden yields produce that's used by the local community. The
building itself is LEED platinum-certified, with half of the facility's power supplied by an onsite wind turbine.

Another lighthouse on the provenance horizon is Everlane,
the ecommerce retailer of "ethical clothing." In six short years,
the startup has grown to over $100 million in revenue, and it's
done so by making its products' provenance radically transparent.[11] That includes publishing the cost structure for its
products. During "Transparency Tuesdays," consumers can
meet and greet with company employees on Instagram. And
by accessing a map on the brand's website, consumers can get
a view into each of the company's factories. Clicking into the
jeans plant reveals that it is "the world's cleanest denim factory," and the company backs up that claim by providing loads
of data and reasons to believe, like air-drying.

Within the food industry, there's been a sweeping turn toward products that are both greener and more transparent. In the fall of 2018, Panera added a new bread featuring 55 percent whole grains, and McDonald's announced that it was removing artificial preservatives, flavors, and colors from its classic burgers. Ahead of those big chains are upstart manufacturers like Pressed Juicery and Plum Organics — vanguards in delivering foods with a cleaner provenance.

As a first step toward activating your creed within your core operations, question your product's provenance:

- What source materials, production locations, or methods are incongruent with our creed?

- In what ways can our product's provenance be more virtuous?

- What operational changes would most effectively telegraph our creed?

- What adjustments to our products' provenance would garner the most goodwill among people who share our values?

Demonstrative Policies

Like "CVS Quits for Good," an operational policy is a powerful way for you to put commitment behind your creed, telegraph your brand's convictions, and earn goodwill. And when that policy has an inherent cost to the company, it sends a powerful signal of virtue. Another example is Chick-fil-A's "cellphone coop." In select markets, a box on each table presents the following "family challenge":

1. Turn all family cellphones to silent and place in this coop.

2. Enjoy your meal and each other distraction free!

3. After the meal, let us know that you have successfully completed the challenge and each of you will be rewarded with an Icedream® cone![12]

While telegraphing the brand's family-oriented values, the cellphone policy has also earned the goodwill of parents, conservative communities, and childhood development experts.

Elsewhere, the Kroger grocery store chain has adopted a policy goal of zero waste. In the interest of "nourishing our communities and preserving our planet," it established an operational "moonshot" to eliminate food loss across its system by 2025. The "Zero Hunger | Zero Waste" program is combined with a cause initiative aimed at eliminating hunger in the communities that the company serves.

Currently, store associates are empowered to identify meat, produce, dairy, and bakery items that are candidates for donation to food banks. Through this "food rescue program" and other efforts, the company provided the equivalent of 325 million fresh meals last year.[13] It's now accelerating that initiative and, at the same time, is investing in supply-chain work to reduce farm-to-fork food loss.[14]

A bold operational choice like this can become a "signature act" for your brand, telegraphing your creed and enhancing public reputation. Because actions speak louder than words, these ongoing, systemic commitments can truly speak volumes. By demonstrating a genuine sacrifice – a harder road traveled and a hit to the bottom line – they win public respect and esteem.

To identify a demonstrative policy for your brand, ask:

• Which activities or outputs of our operations are most incongruent with our creed? If a cynic measured our inner functioning against our purpose and convictions, where would he find shortcomings?

- What operational changes would garner the most goodwill among people who share our values?

- What operational changes would most effectively tele-graph our creed and create buzz in the culture?

Branded Cause Programs

Another way to make an operational commitment to your creed and contribute to social wellbeing is through a branded cause program. Well-known examples include General Mills' "Box Tops for Education" (providing funds to local schools), Yoplait's "Save Lids to Save Lives" (supporting breast cancer research), and Tide "Loads of Hope" (disaster relief). Here are three more benchmarks:

- The purpose of Dulux paint is to "add colour to people's lives." One way that the brand lives out that purpose is through its "Let's Colour Project." The brand acts as a community organizer for large-scale painting projects that visually transform neighborhoods, usually in devel-oping nations. The company also donates the paint — over a million liters worth since 2009. All told, more than eleven thousand volunteers have completed more than two thousand painting projects around the world.[15]

- For fifteen years running, Johnson & Johnson has mounted its "Campaign for Nursing's Future." This initiative stems directly from the company's Credo, which begins: "We believe our first responsibility is to the doctors, nurses and patients . . ." It aims to address a major societal issue in the U.S. — a shortage of nurses. Through advertising, a website, social media activity, resource guides, scholar-ships and more, the company helps with both recruitment and retention. In part due to the company's efforts, the number of nursing graduates has more than doubled since 2002.[16]

- The Huggies diaper brand in Canada built a cause program around its core conviction: "We believe in the power of hugs." The team launched a "No Baby Unhugged" initiative aimed at providing newborns an adequate level of skin-to-skin connection after birth. (Among the many benefits to infants, skin-to-skin connection has been shown to foster weight gain, improve sleep quality, and strengthen immune function.) Part of the program involves a "Hospital Hugging" program, in which certified volunteer huggers give parents a break and give hugs to babies in need. Over the course of three years, promotion of the program turned around a declining business, and in 2016, brand sales grew 27 percent.[17]

Picking a Congruent Cause

There are two ways to adopt a social cause program: create one or join one. With whichever path you choose, the most vital selection criterion is values congruence. Does the cause clearly align with your convictions and prime value? Does it arise from your purpose and bring the world closer to the desired reality you seek? Through your activism, are you "bleeding your creed?"

That alignment is critical to creating the "win-win" that will make your cause support sustainable over time. The more your business benefits, the greater the likelihood of long-term viability. With strong alignment, your cause work will be accretive to your brand, eventually becoming an "owned" business association. Without it, your activism risks coming off as "cause-washing." By way of caution, consider KFC's now-defunct "Buckets for the Cure" campaign, a

---

partnership with the Susan G. Komen initiative to fight breast cancer. In the words of one blogger: "What the cluck?!"

Purposeful Philanthropy

Another approach to making a social contribution is philanthropic giving. But in order to demonstrate integrity, a critical lens must be added: the lens of your creed. Beyond just giving, purposeful philanthropy signals your convictions and moves the world closer to your desired reality. Here are three examples:

- IBM's worldview stems from the company's first president, Thomas Watson, Sr., who said, "Knowledge is the result of thought, and thought is the keynote of success in this business or any business."[18] In keeping with that conviction, IBM's Corporate Service Corps is a pro-bono program through which teams of IBMers solve various civic issues. Launched in 2008, the Service Corps sends a team of eight to fifteen employees into an emerging market, where they spend up to three months working with local leaders to address social and economic problems. Each year, the company dispatches dozens of teams, and to date, it's delivered more than $70 million worth of consultation on over a thousand projects.[19]

- In keeping with its prime value of interdependence, Whole Foods Market offers low-interest loans to local producers, with the aim of helping them grow and thrive. To date, Whole Foods' "Local Producer Loan Program" has made $22 million in loans to independent farmers and food artisans.[20] Through the Whole Foods Foundation, the company also backs other micro-lending organizations, ones that are focused on alleviating poverty. Through its giving, the company estimates it has improved the lives of over a million poor people in 50-plus countries. CEO John Mackey writes, "Probably nothing we have done in our history at Whole Foods Market has raised the morale of the organization more than the work of this foundation."[21]

- From the inception of Warby Parker, the founders (four business school friends) were concerned about lack of access to eyewear. In the developed world, that meant lack of access to fashionable glasses at affordable prices. Looking out to the developing world, the injustice was a billion people without any access to corrective eyewear. So from the start, Warby Parker integrated its selling proposition with philanthropic giving — donating proceeds from every purchase to VisionSpring, a non-profit that propagates eye exams and distributes low-cost eyewear. The related goodwill has helped the company grow into a $1 billion icon in a short eight years.

The Warby Parker example represents the highest form of congruence and commitment. The brand's creed is embedded into the very fiber of the business model. That is to say, the approach goes beyond philanthropy; it is a demonstrative policy. In this way, it represents a gold standard of operationalizing a social commitment with integrity and virtue. It does in spades what any societal intervention must do: authentically "bleed your creed" while making a contribution to society.

Case for Action

- Consumers demand socially responsible behavior. When you deliver against those expectations, your brand garners goodwill. Goodwill helps you land job candidates, motivate employees, and attract customers. It also helps you forge partnerships, lure investors, and mitigate reputation crises.

- The most compelling way to demonstrate social responsibility is by making the commitment deeply operational.

- There are four ways to operationalize a commitment to social responsibility. They are: (1) your product's "provenance," (2) demonstrative policies, (3) branded cause programs, and (4) purposeful philanthropy.

Actions to Take

- Display an operational commitment to your brand's creed, demonstrating integrity in the way you make a social contribution.

- Ensure that there's congruence and virtue in your product's "provenance" — its origins all along the supply chain.

- Adopt demonstrative policies — "signature acts" that exhibit a harder road traveled and a hit to the bottom line.

- Build and sustain a branded cause program.

- Make philanthropic contributions that signal your creed and move the world closer to your desired reality.

CHAPTER 6
Brand with Values

If you would persuade, you must appeal
to interest not intellect.

—Benjamin Franklin

An Evolved Approach to Relevance

Since I first started building brands in the late 90s, there's been a seismic shift in the strategic approach. Prior to that time, the governing concept was "positioning." The goal of positioning is to own a dominant association in consumers' minds, usually a particular feature or attribute. Jif = fresh-roasted peanut taste. Dawn = grease-cutting. Folgers = eye-opening aroma.

But beginning in the 1980s, that all started to change. Leading-edge brands found a higher plane that was more activist than anchored. Nike unleashed human potential; Starbucks cultivated a new "third place" in society; and Patagonia worked to solve the environmental crisis. These were among the vanguard brands with a purpose.

For a while, that approach seemed to be reserved for an elite, special class of brands. That was until a mild soap brand upended the brand-building discipline forever. At the dawn of the new millennium, Dove broke out of its dated, yellowing box and picked a fight with the beauty industry. Launching its "Campaign for Real Beauty," the brand confronted stereotypes in service of its purpose — to help more women feel beautiful every day. A gem in that effort was its "Beauty Sketches" film, in which forensic drawings revealed deficits in how women perceived their own beauty. It became the number-one most viewed online ad of all time.[1]

Dove tore the fabric of the brand-building universe for two reasons. First, it wasn't born with purpose; it adopted it. Secondly, bar soap is about as "low interest" as a category can get. Because of what's often called the "Dove Effect," every brand in every category now has permission to lay claim to purpose, and many have enjoyed similar breakout successes. Products like KIND Snacks and Method cleaning products have elevated "low-involvement" categories into high-interest brands. And many top-performing campaigns have featured everyday brands making extraordinary impacts. In 2014, the Always "Like a Girl" campaign drove measurable shifts in public sensitivity toward the use of that phrase while also generating significant lifts in brand preference and purchase intent.[2]

Today, a purpose- and values-based approach to brand building is the winning formula. The parent of Dove, consumer-goods multinational Unilever, is a microcosm for the shift. While some of the company's brands have been slow to make the evolution, several — like Dove, Lifebuoy, Ben & Jerry's, and Brooke Bond tea — are strongly purpose-driven. In comparing the two groups, the company found that the brands that act on purpose are growing 46 percent faster than the rest of the business. Together, they accounted for 70 percent of the company's growth in 2017.[3] At the level of the parent brand, Unilever is a purpose-driven success in its own right, driving 30 percent revenue growth behind its "Sustainable Living Plan" to reduce environmental impacts while increasing social ones.[4]

These successes reflect an underlying consumer shift: a pivot from "material want" to "meaning want." In their drive for self-expression and connection, more consumers are aligning themselves with companies and brands that share and manifest their personal values. In the words of research powerhouse Millward-Brown, "It's no longer about what people buy; it's about what they buy into."

So it is that a creed fosters brand relevance. In fact, nearly two-thirds of Millennials and Gen Z express a preference for brands that have a point of view and stand for something.[5] They seek not only physical value but also "metaphysical" value. In their experience of the brand, they want to know, not only what a product does, but also how its provider *thinks*. What's the company's philosophy with regard to supply and manufacturing? How does it treat its employees? In their heart of hearts, what do the leaders really care about? What are their deepest values and intentions? Are they only in it for the cash?

A study by Edelman highlights the sea change. It found that "consumers are now just as likely to express purchase intent based on a brand's values as they are based on the features of a product."[6] They assess that nearly two out of three consumers are "belief-driven buyers" — those who buy based on a brand's stand.[7]

In another body of research, Pixability found that consumers have higher engagement with ads that support social values.[8] Meanwhile, research powerhouse Millward-Brown reports, "Analysis of key brands in the Top 100 over the past decade shows that brands with a stronger purpose — that is, brands that are perceived to make consumers' lives better and seem to put purpose before profit — also create greater brand equity."[9]

What this represents is a third phase of market evolution, what marketing authority Philip Kotler terms "Marketing 3.0." The first phase emphasized 'function' — the rational aspects of a product. The second focused on 'emotions' — the feelings that a brand evokes. In the third phase, the priority is shared values — the fulfillment of human aspirations. In phase one, Dove soap moisturized skin. In phase two, the brand pampered women and made them feel more beautiful. In phase three, Dove is a catalyst for advancing the self-esteem of all women.

For brands, this approach represents a more durable form of competitive distinction. In a world where product features are readily copied, adopting a point of view provides a more sustainable source of difference. Ogilvy Advertising examined this opportunity, and then-CEO Miles Young reported, "We've looked at brands that have a strong point of view vs. brands that don't, and you can see a clear differentiation in brand imagery and consumer bonding translated into market share."[10]

The Magnetic Power of Values

One of the principal business advantages of this branding approach is the organic draw created by "conviction attraction." A strong point of view innately lures new customers to your business. Strong convictions generate interest and invite engagement.

That's because convictions are inherently attracting. Throughout human history, we've been drawn to resolute voices, whether it was that of Julius Caesar in the Roman Forum, Teddy Roosevelt on his "bully pulpit," or Gloria Steinem on *Meet the Press.* The driver, according to emotional intelligence guru Travis Bradberry, is the mirror neurons in our brains. They mirror the emotional state of others, and our brains like the certainty we see.[11] It's this same effect that causes us to trust companies and brands that display a strong point of view. As the saying goes, passion is persuasive.

There's another behavioral force at work here — our human drive to scrutinize intentionality. In order to survive, our ancestors had to make judgments about the motives of others. Our brains are wired to look for cues to others' intentions, and we're really good at interpreting subtleties. Because of this evolutionary preset, your customers' brains are chemically rewarded when they get a sense of the "why" that governs your company's actions. As Simon Sinek asserted in his famous TED Talk "Start with Why," "People don't buy what you do; they buy why you do it."[12]

Not surprisingly, Steve Jobs had this all figured out a couple decades ago. In 1997, he gave a master class on the power of sharing convictions. The occasion was the launch of Apple's iconic "Think Different" campaign, and he took to the stage to debut the TV spot for an internal audience. Leaning against the podium in a long-sleeve black shirt, shorts and sandals, he began by saying, "To me, marketing is about values. This is a very complicated world. It's a very noisy world. And we're not going to get a chance to get people to remember much about us. No company is. And so we have to be really clear on what we want them to know about us."

Pressing his hands together pensively, he contended, "Our customers want to know: who is Apple, and what is it that we stand for? Where do we fit in this world?"

He answered in this way:

> What we're about isn't making boxes for people to get their jobs done – although we do that well. We do that better than almost anybody in some cases. But Apple is about something more than that. Apple at the core – its core value is that, we believe that people with passion can change the world for the better. That's what we believe . . . And that those people who are crazy enough to think that they can change the world, are the ones that actually do.[13]

In essence, he declared that Apple's point of view resides squarely in quadrant D – the world of originality and breaking conventions.

At the conclusion of his remarks, Jobs cued one of the most powerful ads ever made. Featuring "rebels" like Einstein, Lennon and Gandhi – and a pitch-perfect voiceover by Richard Dreyfuss – it was a moving expression of the creed that moves Apple.

Twenty years later, it's more critical than ever that you assert your brand's creed. It's what customers want from you. In fact, today, a full 87 percent of U.S. consumers say they consider a brand's values when making a purchase.[14] In part, it's how they manifest their self-concepts. They align themselves with brands that reflect and sustain their personal points of view. As an illustration, consider the values sync that's on display when someone hangs this popular Disney poster on his or her wall:

> *In this house*
> *we let it go*
> *Because Hakuna Matata*

and all the Bear Necessities
will always be our guide
To infinity and beyond
All it takes is faith, trust
and a little bit of pixie dust
We believe in happy endings
And we know that
life is always better under the sea
Because in this house
we do Disney

From a business point of view, these values hooks have immeasurable value, particularly given how difficult it is to engage consumers today. It's well established that "push" marketing has hit the wall and a new "earned" era now reigns. As marketing consultant JP Kuehlwein writes, "Brands can no longer force their way into existing content and discourse, they must become the content and initiate the discourse themselves, attractive enough for people to rally around, connect and engage with."[15]

In this new paradigm, product-related content will rarely become the nexus for participation. In order to earn advocacy, companies and brands need to engage on a higher level. Life-level convictions are that discourse-driving stuff. Convictions and values are the currency for active consumer engagement.

For inspiration, we can look to Milwaukee-based Harley-Davidson. Harley-Davidson's business is on a down cycle (pun intended), but there can be no doubt that the company has built one of the world's most compelling brands. It's a communing point for a collective belief system.

Harley-Davidson articulated that belief system in a two-minute film called "Live By It." Backed by a smoky electric-guitar track, the black-and-white video depicts a swelling road rally, and a chorus of biker voices recites their creed. The opening lines are:

> We believe in going our own way — no matter which way the rest of the world is going.

> We believe in bucking the system that's built to smash individuals like bugs on a windshield.

> Some of us believe in the man upstairs; all of us believe in sticking it to the man down here.[16]

When a rider buys a Harley, he isn't buying a bike. He's joining a rebellion movement that has taken up loud engines instead of arms. He dons the black-leather uniform and the militaristic insignia of an insurgency.

Within this creed-fueled militia has arisen one of the world's largest community-marketing programs: the Harley Owners Group. With over a million members, its chapters self-organize to engage fellow riders in rallies, on the road and off.[17] Of all the engines powering the Harley business, none has more torque than the "HOG."

Creed-fired brands spend surprisingly little on marketing. Advocacy replaces advertising. We see examples across diverse industries:

- As I described in Chapter 4, the experience of grace at Chick-fil-A has produced a legion of hardcore fans. Because of their loyalty and advocacy, the company doesn't need a lot of marketing investment. While McDonald's spends 2.6 percent of gross revenue on advertising, Chick-fil-A spends only 0.84 percent.[18]

- Lush Cosmetics has grown steadily for twenty years. The company's creed focuses on the provenance of its products, including a commitment to sourcing fresh, organic ingredients and to never testing on animals. Drafting from their operating principles, the company has taken a strong stance against animal cruelty, which in turn has engendered the active support of brand fans on social media. Buoyed by that support, Lush has sustained its 20-year climb without spending a dime on above- or below-the-line promotions.[19]

Conviction Attraction in the B2B World

A strong point of view may be a magnet for retail consumers, but does it work in the B2B world too? In fact, it does. When product and price are parity, a point of view can provide preference-driving distinction. According to best-practice insights firm CEB, 58 percent of small-business owners would pick one supplier over another if that supplier demonstrated more support of moral and social values.[20]

As a case in point, consider Hiscox insurance, which was named the 2018 Small Corporate Marketer of the Year by the Association of National Advertisers (ANA). Although Hiscox is a relative newcomer in the U.S., the company has made big gains in recent years, including a five-fold increase in unaided awareness and a sizable jump in brand affinity.[21] It's done so with a conviction: "When you are courageous, things that seemed impossible are possible." Having previously defined itself as an "insurance" business, Hiscox is now in the "courage" business. Its stated purpose is "to help the courageous overcome the impossible," and its corporate tagline is "Encourage Courage." As we've seen at other conviction-powered firms, the commitment to courage starts inside. According to CMO Russ Findlay, "Hiscox encourages courage among all of its employees, and challenges them to challenge convention, to take the status quo and question it."[22] In market, its "I'mpossible" campaign features inspirational stories of start-ups, and it launched with a high-profile provocation: a full-page ad in the *Wall Street Journal* headlined "Has America lost its courage?" It cut through the clutter of the conservative B2B insurance world.

So how do you activate "conviction attraction" on your brand? There are two branding levers that will signal your convictions to the world. They are: markers with meaning and public statements of creed. Through these devices, you and your brand can effectively "bleed your creed."

Markers with Meaning

One way to generate conviction attraction is to "bleed your creed" through your brand's identifiers, which may include your logotype, icon, colors, shape, pattern, jingle, or spokes-character. These markers are foundational to the work of standing out and standing for something. In all the various permutations of your business and all its myriad actions, they provide the "executional sameness" that allows people to form impressions of your enterprise and repeatedly engage with it as a known and familiar entity. Here's how brand identifiers work:

Think of your brain as a library. Within it, there are stacks and stacks of books — each one dedicated to a particular topic and filled with imprinted memories, feelings and associations. In one corner of the library is a section called 'brands,' and for each of the brands you know, there's a dedicated volume. Like every other book, it's filled with associations and emotions.

Every now and again, your brain goes to the stacks to retrieve a particular brand, either to fill it with a new impression or to check its contents when you're considering a purchase. To find the book, your neural processor rapidly scans the shelves, perusing the spines. How readily it finds the book depends on how prominent the book and its markings are on the shelf.

As an example, think about soft-drink brands. For most of us, the Coca-Cola book is easy to find in our brains. When we think of the category, Coke is front and center on the shelf, the spine of the book is thick, and the cover is all red (PMS #484) with the title written in a familiar white script. Ask your neural processor to find the book on Sierra Mist and it will have to search a little harder.

In many ways, the work of brand building is fairly simple: create strong executional assets, present them ubiquitously, and fill them with meaning. That's one of the principal conclusions of author Byron Sharp in his book *How Brands Grow*. He argues that repeated exposure to distinctive brand assets builds strong memory structures, which in turn support habitual purchase. According to his research, this is a reliable lever for lifting market share in mature categories.[23]

For creed-fueled brands, there's another dimension at play here: how effectively the executional markers advance your point of view and facilitate the embedding of related associations. Different than having recognizable assets just for recognition sake, the markers of a creed-inspired enterprise are symbols of a meaning system. Your "book" has to have rich stuff inside it – a premise, conflict, and a moral – and your identifiers need to carry that mantle. They must telegraph and support the plotline. McDonald's would have a difficult time standing for joy if its arches were gray.

There are many examples of creed-fired brands with great markers, but none greater than Harley-Davidson. As a symbol of rebellion, what better icon than a militaristic coat of arms? Combined with black leather, flames and skulls, and rumbling engines, the markings of Harley promise a gritty story about an insurgency.

If you're a new brand, the opportunity begins with the brand name itself. Your name can be an open declaration of intent – like the one Jessica Alba adopted when she founded The Honest Company. Or the meaning can be veiled – a revelation to be discovered. Such is the case of Sugru, a moldable glue product developed by designer Jane Ni Dhulchaointigh. Her creatively inspired brand takes its name from the Irish word for "play."

Because our brains are so adept at visual processing, colors and logos are powerful vessels for conveying meaning. The charging red bulls on your favorite energy drink are strongly emblematic of vitality and challenge. Airbnb's "Bélo" logo is a thoughtfully crafted symbol of belonging, connoting a location pin, a heart, and being "in the loop."[24] In the year 2000, Johnnie Walker turned around its legacy "striding man" so he moved forward (to the right) as an icon of progress. Recently, Kleenex animated its logotype so that the "e's" join up together, symbolizing the brand's prime value of connection.

For your brand to effectively convey its creed, these executional identifiers are foundational. They transmit your unique point of view and serve as the "cover art" for the volume of associations that consumers aggregate in their mental libraries. The more representative your cover art is, the more readily your creed will get imprinted.

Public Statements of Creed

The most overt way to generate conviction attraction is to present your point of view in your external communications. Whether that's a singular anthem film or an ongoing campaign, every brand can attract fans by pronouncing its creed openly and explicitly. One way to do that is through your posted, printed and digital communications. At Pirch's retail locations, the brand's "Live Joyfully" creed is prominently displayed on the walls. Yeti's product catalog is a celebration of adventure. And Marucci (the baseball equipment manufacturer) has a webpage dedicated to its prime value of commitment. The page features the brand's creed and videos of marquee athletes espousing the brand's ideals. (The manifestos of both Yeti and Marucci appear in Appendix D).

Your creed can also be the crux of your branding campaign. Here are three examples:

- Since the early 2000s, the Michigan Economic Development Corporation has built that state's tourism campaign around the prime value of purity. Its radio campaign celebrates that human ideal, capturing vignettes of pure experiences in the state. Each ad features the clear-timbered voice of actor and Michigan native Tim Allen. A classic is "Snow Day": "When the schools were closed and the day was wide open / the first step into fresh powder was like stepping into a new world." During one four-year study period, the campaign generated almost four million additional visitors, who spent almost a billion dollars in the state. For every $1 spent in media, the state realized $2.82 in tourism revenue.[25]

- In recent years, Adidas has found great success by reclaiming its ethos of originality. A video for its "Originals" sub-brand featured a remake of Frank Sinatra's classic "My Way," with next-gen musicians like Dev Hynes, Stormzy, and Dej Loaf taking the song to their own unique place. The moral of the campaign: "Original is Never Finished." During the campaign period, U.S. sales rose 85 percent.[26]

- Faced with challenging business dynamics and an oppositional political climate, *The New York Times* launched a campaign in February 2017 aimed at defending its prime value of truth. Called "The Truth is Hard," it underscored the subjectivity of opinions and asserted the brand's commitment to truthful reporting. The campaign celebrated the depth of the *Times'* journalism bench and the difficult, on-the-ground work that reporters do. One execution highlighted how, through their work, reporters are shining a light on gender inequities around the world. On the heels of the campaign launch, the brand experienced the strongest growth in subscriptions in six years.[27]

Case for Action

- There's been a seismic shift in the way brands create relevance. This evolution is a response to a consumer pivot from "material want" to "meaning want." In their experience of your brand, consumers want to know not only what your product does but also how your organization *thinks*.

- By embracing a creed-inspired approach, you will gain the business benefit of "conviction attraction." Because passion is persuasive, a strong point of view creates a beacon, stirring interest far and wide. It also spawns advocates who become "media" for your brand.

Actions to Take

- Signal your brand's creed through your brand's identifiers: your logotype, icon, colors, shape, pattern, jingle, and spokescharacter. These markers should be designed to express your point of view and facilitate the embedding of related associations.

- Make public statements of your point of view. You can do that through your posted, printed and digital communications or by making your creed the centerpiece of your branding campaign.

CHAPTER 7

Be a Protagonist

Everyone is entitled to my opinion. —*Madonna*

Making Cultural Waves

It's hard to overstate the enormity of change that has reshaped the function of marketing over the last couple decades. Fragmentation of media has made it nearly impossible to purchase mass awareness, and consumers actively fend off ads with every tech tool available to them. At the same time, social networks have risen up to become the arbiters of preference, molding the narrative about brands — outside the direct control of corporate image-makers.

Yet, your mandate as a brand builder remains unchanged: to grow your brand, you have to garner meaningful attention. You have to become more "mentally available," forging a distinctive impression in consumers' minds. In other words, you have to simultaneously stand *out* and stand *for* something.

In this context, the seam between brands and popular culture has become almost fully fused. The two forces have always abutted, but in the new "earned era," that relationship is more interdependent than ever. To get the meaningful attention that's needed for growth, your brand needs to be part of the cultural conversation. It needs to be picked up by social media and carried aloft. It needs the active participation and engagement of advocates.

As an illustration of the power of cultural currents, let's return to the summer of the Ice Bucket Challenge. In June of 2014, a few prognosticators on the Golf Channel dumped frigid water over their heads to promote awareness for ALS disease. The exhilarating campaign quickly moved to Facebook, and each person who did the stunt uploaded a video of it, laying down a challenge for someone (or some others) to follow suit. If the named person failed to comply — as President Obama did — they were encouraged to make a donation to support ALS research.

The campaign generated a massive cultural wave of ice-cold water. During the course of July and August, over three million people — including virtually every celebrity figure — posted videos of themselves conducting the bone-chilling act. Plenty of others didn't, and as a result, the ALS Association saw a 3,500 percent spike in donations.[1]

The Ice Bucket Challenge represents something I call "protagonism." (It's a legitimate English word, but it doesn't get much usage.) A protagonist is a proponent for a cause, an advocate – the leader of a movement. It comes from the Greek *protagonistes*, meaning "actor who plays the chief or first part." Protagonism, then, is about leadership – opening hearts and minds, inspiring action, provoking positive change. Protagonism gets people engaged and talking, and it moves the world closer to a desired end state.

Historically, some of the most effective ads have been acts of protagonism. Here's a brief survey:

- In the 1950s, VW provoked people to "Think Small."

- In the 60s, Virginia Slims instigated women's libbers to smoke freely and proudly, declaring, "You've Come a Long Way."

- In the 70s, a crying Indian impelled Americans to stop littering.

- In the 80s, Nike started fomenting would-be athletes to "Just Do It."

- In the 90s, Apple incited us to "Think Different."

- In the 2000s, Dove's "Evolution" challenged our artificial standards of beauty.

This decade, Patagonia tweaked our environmental consciousness by admonishing, "Don't Buy This Jacket." On Black Friday 2011, the company took out a full-page ad in *The New York Times*, highlighting the environmental toll that a single jacket exacts during its production. With that, the company inaugurated its "Common Threads Initiative" encouraging repair and reuse. Today, through its "Worn Wear" program, the company facilitates repair and encourages reuse via an online used-clothing store.

Today, protagonism is more of a mandate than ever before. Branding guru Martin Lindstrom writes:

> The fact is that consumers are tiring of perfectly polished brands. Inoffensive brands. Brands essentially without opinions or courage. Bland brands. That's why brands increasingly need to take a stand on issues, to express their values and opinions, and demonstrate responsibility towards them. Brands without well-defined opinions will find it increasingly difficult to gain traction in the marketplace.[2]

As Martin advises, your brand needs to be forceful, emphatic and resolute. It needs to rise up out of the cultural waters and have a voice in the public conversation. It's the most effective and efficient way to gain the attention that your topline needs.

According to research by Edelman, consumers are more likely to advocate for a brand after hearing about its stand (32 percent) than its product features (26 percent).[3] In other words, the world wants to hear about your brand's creed. So express it to the culture by making some waves.

Shifting Cultural Contexts

In order to capture cultural attention, brands need to rise with the flows of the zeitgeist. Popular culture is like an ocean upon which all of society and its institutions float, and on that vast body of undulating energy, companies and brands are like ships, pushed along by powerful currents. How much cultural attention your brand is able to garner has everything to do with these movements. Some brands get a big lift by catching a well-aligned wave. That is, they ride the energy of a cultural movement. Other times, a brand makes a splash by pushing against a wave or creating one of its own.

Riding a Cultural Wave

In the ocean of culture, there are giant swells that come along every now and then and move all of society. In the U.S. in the 1960s, there was the civil rights movement, followed by the peace movement in the 70s. While the 80s was a decade of feel-good buoyancy, the 90s saw grunge and street values surge. As each wave of culture crests, a well-linked brand promotion can rise with it, enhancing the brand's prominence and relevance.

Today, a dominant cultural value is female empowerment. An analysis by ad tech company Pixability found that, for Interbrand's Top 100 brands in 2016, this was the most common topic among all purpose-driven ads (24 percent of the total).[4] Among the many brands that caught that wave, one of the most successful was financial services firm State Street, which molded and installed the "Fearless Girl" statue on Wall Street. Facing off against the famous bronze "Charging Bull," the statue was an act of protagonism, advocating for more women to hold seats on corporate boards. It soon became a powerful symbol of female empowerment and a popular New York tourist attraction. Within three months of installation, State Street's share of voice shot up from 7.8 percent to 37.4 percent, and with that, a small piece of hard-content advertising (which cost $250,000 to produce) delivered a marketing value worth more than $25 million in impressions.[5]

Over the last few years, there have been a host of other surfers trying to catch the female empowerment wave. REI celebrated women in a "Force of Nature" campaign. McDonald's marked International Women's Day by turning its arches upside down on all of its digital channels. And Johnnie Walker introduced a Jane Walker label.

Unfortunately, many of these efforts left the culture cold. In its coverage of the Jane Walker initiative, CNN reported on a social media backlash, quoting one woman who said, "I don't see this as a symbol of gender equality; all I see is a marketing strategy to increase sales."[6]

As that example highlights, not every cultural wave is right for every brand. The temptation is high: 86 percent of consumers say they like it when a brand takes a stand for social issues.[7] But when the prime value of the brand doesn't match the prime value of the movement, it feels like the brand is co-opting the issue for commercial gain. Implicitly, the culture understands that the brand's true protagonism lies elsewhere, so its involvement smells like borrowed interest.

As every good surfer knows, not every wave has the right energy and direction. Sometimes it's better to wait for another wave.

Resisting Opposing Forces

When a brand has a strong point of view, it can readily spot cultural currents that run contrary to its creed. And when it stands up against those menaces, it telegraphs its convictions and attains greater cultural significance.

Over the last several decades, no brand has embodied this approach more powerfully and consistently than Coke. The brand is an unrelenting protagonist for unity and goodwill, and time and again, it has faced up against issues that threaten its view of a better world:

- In 1969, the company ran a print ad depicting a group of boys sitting together on a bench, happily enjoying their Cokes. On closer inspection, the bench is an artifact of segregation, with a bar dividing it into two sections. Sitting shoulder to shoulder, there are two black boys and one white boy interspersed on each side, blissfully ignorant of the partitions.

- In the early 1970s, the brand responded to post-Vietnam War strife with its iconic "Hilltop" ad — an ode to global harmony.

- The brand's 2007 Super Bowl spot reinvented the darkly controversial *Grand Theft Auto* video game into a vehicle of love.

- During the 2014 Super Bowl, as U.S. culture grappled with immigration and marriage equality, Coke took to the air with "America the Beautiful" — a panoramic celebration of American diversity.

Pop-cultural resonance is a primary reason that Coke has sustained its iconic power for decades. By continually standing up against oppositional currents, the brand consistently stands out, deepening the story in our minds. Today, the brand faces an anti-sugar wave that may submerge it; but there can be no denying the brilliance of its brand-building history — and the power of defending a definitive point of view.

Being a protagonist means voicing your point of view. It means asserting your opinion into the pop-cultural conversation. By so doing, your marketing activations effectively "bleed your creed."

In order to catch and make cultural waves, you can adopt three types of protagonism: (1) cause-driven, (2) policy-based, and (3) socio-political. Each one reflects a successively higher dependence on the cultural zeitgeist and comes with more risk. The first derives from an identified social need inspired by your creed. The second approach bucks against a perceived problem in the marketplace or culture. The last interjects the brand into a social or political conversation that's prevalent in the contemporary culture.

	Cause-driven Protagonism	Policy-based Protagonism	Socio-political Protagonism
Example	ALS Ice Bucket Challenge	Patagonia Common Treads/ Worn Wear	State Street Fearless Girl
Dependence on the Cultural Zeitgeist	Low	Mid	High
Political Risk to the Business or Brand	Low	Mid	High

Cause-Driven Protagonism

Irrespective of the dominant cultural wave patterns, your brand can garner attention by fomenting a movement of its own. As in the example of the Ice Bucket Challenge, you can drop your own metaphorical rock in the water and help it ripple throughout the culture. A movement of this type will derive from an identified social need. Here are three examples:

- In the late 1990s, U.K. laundry detergent Persil adopted the conviction that "dirt is good." Armed with loads of data showing that kids need more unstructured time in nature, the brand became a protagonist for outdoor play. (And, don't worry, its product will take care of the stains.) Over the course of thirteen years, that posture helped to grow global sales more than ten times. In 2016, the brand reignited the movement in the U.K. by bringing fresh urgency to the crusade. A viral video dramatized a frightening reality: the average kid spends less time outdoors than a prison inmate does. The culture responded with urgency, boosting both the brand's popularity and the number of hours that school kids spend outside.[8]

- In 2010, American Express started a movement on the conviction that, "for communities to thrive, small businesses need to thrive." It created a national holiday called "Small Business Saturday" — falling in between Black Friday and Cyber Monday — and encouraged the public to support local merchants. Each year, the movement drives a wave of consumer action, and in 2017, over 40 percent of Americans reported visiting independent shops that day, dropping billions of dollars along the way.[9]

- In 2014, Seventh Generation campaigned for a bill that would strengthen chemical safety regulations. On Earth Day, the company took out a full-page ad in *The New York Times*, soliciting signatories to a petition. According to CEO Joey Bergstein, that act of cause support did more for sales of its products than all of its coupons generated that year.[10]

Being a protagonist for a cause starts with identifying a creed-relevant need in society. Aristotle offered this incitement: "Where your talents and the needs of the world cross; there lies your calling." What injustice does your brand see in the world? What societal wrong does it want to right? Therein lies your cause-related protagonism.

Policy-Based Protagonism

In the U.S., Black Friday is a cultural event on par with the Super Bowl. For many shoppers, it's a game they wouldn't miss. Others despise the commercial invasion into their holiday season. In 2015, the outdoor gear retailer REI started putting its own spin on the day. The company announced that all 143 of its retail locations would remain closed that day and its twelve thousand employees would get a paid day off. The implicit attack on consumerism made headlines, but it was the company's companion campaign that packed the real punch.

Dubbed #OptOutside, the store closing launched a movement to get friends and relatives to spend the day after Thanksgiving outdoors together. In a statement, president and CEO Jerry Stritzke said, "Black Friday is the perfect time to remind ourselves of the essential truth that life is richer, more connected and complete when you choose to spend it outside."[11]

The roots of the #OptOutside movement grew out of the philosophy of the co-op's co-founders, Lloyd and Mary Anderson. In a letter to co-op members in 2015, Stritzke articulated the company's governing point of view:

> We believe an outdoor life is a life well lived. That single, simple idea unites our community, no matter where you're from or what your political beliefs are. Seeking adventure and finding ourselves in the outdoors drives a virtuous cycle. We believe that life outside is better for us as individuals, better for society and ultimately, better for the planet. That is what unites us at REI.[12]

That conviction inspired the company and its marketing agencies as they considered ways to address a business need: increasing engagement among younger consumers. Coupled with the insight that among the brand's core audience there was growing contempt for Black Friday, #OptOutside was born.

The cultural response to the campaign was bigger than the company expected. It generated 33 consecutive days of press coverage and over a billion social media impressions, leading over a million people to go to the company's website to sign on to the movement. Despite being on the sidelines for retail's biggest day of the year, the company posted record revenue.[13]

This was not a one-off for the company. It maintains its

policy of a Black Friday shutdown, and in 2016, it expanded its coalition of advocates to include numerous eco-friendly groups and corporations like Subaru.

REI's #OptOutside is an example of protagonism that's driven by an internal policy. That internal policy seeks to buck against a perceived threat to the brand's point of view and purpose. In addressing the threat, the brand takes demonstrative action.

Another example is "CVS Quits for Good." When the company kicked its tobacco habit in 2014, it coupled the policy move with a full-blown anti-smoking campaign. The integrated marketing program drove more than 500,000 people to CVS's smoking cessation hub, and 260,000 would-be quitters sought advice in store.[14]

Policy-driven protagonism starts with a demonstrative act — one that arises from your brand's point of view. To identify that act, ask yourself:

- What are cultural or marketplace threats to our prime value that we should buck against?

- What bold action would provide concrete evidence of our convictions?

Once you've got a substantive policy change to sink your teeth into, turn it into a movement. Make it a cause worth joining. Invest big, and get maximum bang for your bucking.

Socio-Political Protagonism

The last form of protagonism is the gutsiest and grittiest one. It requires you to confront the cultural zeitgeist and assert your point of view. Almost necessarily, that engagement will be politically charged.

An example is Nike's embrace of Colin Kaepernick, the NFL

player who knelt during the National Anthem to protest racial injustice. In a controversial act of protagonism, the brand made Kaepernick the face of its thirtieth anniversary "Just Do It" campaign. The action immediately drew a caustic response from the conservative end of the political spectrum, led by the nation's chief executive. But for most, the move had innate resonance – it aligned with the brand's historical support for athletes and their dreams – and a core audience of urban youth stood ready to lend its fervent support. The socio-political clash fueled broad cultural attention and fired up an army of advocates. Nike saw gains in both short-term sales and long-term measures of brand strength, and after a brief dip, the company's stock made a steady climb.

Acting as a socio-political protagonist is a high-risk, high-reward proposition. Conservatively, Nike realized at least $200 million in media value from its move and made big gains in brand relevance among its target. But not every act of socio-political protagonism has turned out that well. Many brands have gotten badly burned. Consider the case of Keurig:

In November 2017, Keurig announced that it was pulling its ads off Sean Hannity's program on Fox News. The company made the move to protest the host's defense of U.S. Senate candidate Roy Moore, who was accused of sexual misconduct. Within hours, the company was overwhelmed by outrage from Fox viewers, who posted videos of people destroying their coffee makers and launched a #BoycottKeurig movement.

Unlike Nike, Keurig had no innate authority to condemn the candidate, whose criminal acts were unproven; and Keurig's core loyalists had no particular stake in the fight. As a result, the company quickly found itself out of its element. There was no army of loyalists to defend the brand and offset the boycott with increased sales. Absent any real devotion – no native point of view on the matter — Keurig's CEO pulled back its activism and issued an apology.

Looking across the field of political hits and misses, one success factor is clear: congruence with the brand's creed. When socio-political protagonism works, it's because the brand has the moral authority to make the stand. Here are three examples:

- Ben & Jerry's is well known for its open and tolerant world-view. So it was a natural to wade into Australia's national debate over legalizing marriage equality. Making a bit of a policy play, the brand banned the sale of two scoops of the same flavor — symbolizing the lack of choice that same-sex couples experienced. Until Australia changed its laws, there would be no same-sex marriage and no same-flavor scoops. In December 2017, the country's marriage equality law passed Parliament in a landslide vote.

- Within the ʻohana (family) culture of Salesforce, one of the four core values is to "drive equality for all people." So alarm bells went off in the company headquarters when Indiana legislators enacted a "religious freedom" law that many feared would allow discrimination against the LGBT population. CEO Marc Benioff voiced strong opposition to the law and, taking forceful action against the state, he initiated a program to relocate the company's Indiana-based employees. Many people inside and outside of Salesforce admired the strength of Benioff's response, and bowing to expanding pressure, the Indiana legislature amended the law to protect LGBT people.

- In 2017, Patagonia mounted a high-profile protest against President Trump's executive order reducing the size of Utah's Bears Ears and Grand Staircase-Escalante National

Monuments. It was a direct affront to the brand's prime value of environmentalism. During the height of the Christmas holiday shopping season, the brand turned its website into a protest billboard. On a solid black homepage, it posted, "The President Stole Your Land." Compared to the more tepid objections of other outdoor apparel brands, Patagonia won fans for the strength of its protagonism. Traffic to the site overwhelmed the company's servers.[15]

Weighing Whether to Enter the Political Fray

Entering the socio-political discourse is delicate and tricky business. On the one hand, two-thirds of U.S. consumers want companies to stand up for what they believe politically.[16] On the other hand, 58 percent of them think companies should stay out of politics.[17]

While those two data points may seem at odds, the nuance in the phrasings helps to explain the cultural context. As is the case with riding a cultural movement, consumers seem to understand (better than business leaders perhaps) that there's a time and place for brand activism. When an issue relates directly to a brand's prime value — its central protagonism — it's expected that the brand will get involved. When it's not, consumers don't want their brands meddling in extraneous affairs. There are already enough highly charged particles in the political atmosphere.

In the end, the most helpful guidance probably comes from Thomas Jefferson, who said, "In matters of style, swim with the current; in matters of principle, stand like a rock."

Taking a strong socio-political stand can be a powerful play for your brand. It can assert your creed, generate engagement, build brand relevance, and advance your purposeful agenda. But before wading into the charged arena of socio-politics, be sure you've got the right moral authority and purposeful resolve, know that backlash comes with the territory, and be prepared to stick to your guns.

Case for Action

- To get the meaningful attention that's required for growth, your brand needs to be part of the pop-cultural conversation. You need social media to pick up your brand and carry it aloft. You need the participatory support of advocates.

- This requires that you engage in "protagonism" — opening hearts and minds to spur positive change, moving the world closer to your desired end state.

- To garner attention in the culture, you should seek to leverage movements. One approach is to ride a cultural wave. As a cultural tide crests, a well-linked brand campaign can rise with it, enhancing the brand's prominence and relevance. Another approach is to stand out by standing up against an opposing force. A third is to make a wave of your own.

Actions to Take

- Engage in cause-driven protagonism by identifying a social need inspired by your creed and then fomenting a movement that catalyzes change.

- Engage in policy-based protagonism by bucking against a perceived problem in the marketplace or culture. Use a demonstrative act – a substantive policy change – as the platform for a movement that engages consumers.

- Engage in socio-political protagonism by interjecting your brand into a social or political topic that's prevalent in the contemporary culture.

Conclusion

I began this book with an anecdote about Abraham Lincoln, who demonstrated "the earnestness of a heart convinced" as he mounted his opposition to slavery. As it turns out, Lincoln valued that same devotion to cause in others. On July 6, 1852, he delivered a eulogy for Senator Henry Clay, saying, "Mr. Clay's predominant sentiment, from first to last, was a deep devotion to the cause of human liberty – a strong sympathy with the oppressed everywhere, and an ardent wish for their elevation. With him, this was a primary and all-controlling passion. Subsidiary to this was the conduct of his whole life."[1]

When I work with brands, I often use the frame of a eulogy to interrogate the team's driving purpose and desired impact. If the brand ceased to exist, what would its legacy be? Did it attain a certain market share position? Did it hit a particular revenue level?

As I argued in the Introduction, the most successful businesses would be eulogized along the lines of Lincoln's tribute to Henry Clay:

- The brand had a deep devotion to a cause.

- The cause was its primary and all-consuming passion.

- Subsidiary to that cause was the conduct of its entire activity system.

- *As an outcome,* the brand achieved remarkable business results.

As the culture has fully acknowledged now, purpose can be a transformational force in the lives of people and the course of businesses. But its true power is only unleashed when it represents a heartfelt devotion arising from an authentic point of view. Without genuine intentionality, purpose is a platitude; but with true conviction behind it, purpose can change the world.

As a 20-year veteran of brand building and purposology, that is my core conviction — the one that motivated me to write this book. I firmly believe that a brand will only move the world to the degree that its stewards are moved by the brand's purpose and the convictions that underlie it. As you close this book, I hope you believe that too.

Once an organization is working on purpose, I'm often asked, "How do we know if we're succeeding? What are the measures?"

My answer is the "five opportunities":

- *Are your employees more engaged?* Are you growing the size and shape of your organization's heart? Are you effectively building an internal culture in which every employee is fully aligned to the brand's purpose and convictions?

- *Is your enterprise producing more value for consumers?* Are you using the lens of purpose to innovate offerings that set your brand apart? Are you growing across platforms and deepening the emotional appeal of your proposition?

- *Is your enterprise making social contributions that are truly meaningful?* Have you made your societal commitments deeply operational — in your product's provenance, through your brand's policies, in your cause programs and philanthropy?

- *Is your brand growing relevance?* Are you effectively telegraphing your organization's driving intent through your brand identity (markers, posted statements, and campaigns)?

- *Is your brand garnering more consumer attention?* Are you making waves in the popular culture, spurring positive change and moving the world closer to the brand's desired end state?

If you're making progress in those areas, your organization and your brand are effectively bleeding a creed. As a leader, you've overcome the "purpose challenge," and your business is likely experiencing success. Most significantly, your enterprise is changing the world.

Acknowledgments

This book is about the power of conviction. Although I've written about it in a business context, that power can be felt in our personal lives as well. In fact, I think one of the greatest gifts that anyone can give is to say, "I believe in you." I'm profoundly grateful to the people who believed in me and believed in this work.

The first on that list are my "believers-in-chief," my mom and dad – to whom I've dedicated this book. It is my firm conviction that they are two of the best human beings that the world has recently known. Growing up in their home, I was graced by their deep wisdom, seemingly boundless generosity and constant good cheer; but the greatest gift they gave me was their unconditional love. For that, I'm eternally grateful.

Sadly, my mom passed away just as this book was going into production. She was a model of kindness and virtue, and her beautifully radiant heart lit up every room. I will miss her light in my life but will forever feel the warmth of her sunny, loving spirit.

In my career at P&G, I was blessed to have the support of some truly remarkable mentors. Maureen Hood brought me into the company and supported my immersion into brand strategy. Mike Schafer taught me invaluable lessons about leadership and life. With his awesome talent, heart and humor, Brad Wadler serially produced some of the most gratifying and fun-filled days of my life. Leonora Polonsky gave me a "pinch-me" job opportunity, with daily access to her keen strategic mind. A true master of capability building, Lisa Hillenbrand helped me build mine; and Daniel Epstein stretched my capacity and consciousness in ways that few others have. I'm deeply indebted to all of them.

As the cliché accurately goes, P&G's greatest strength is its people, and at every turn, I had the tremendous good fortune to work with brilliant, principled and uplifting colleagues who made me a better person and businessperson. There are too many BBIC, agency, R&D, brand and design friends to name, but you know who you are.

I'm also grateful to the early champions of purpose at P&G. They believed in me and in my work and were essential partners. Foremost on that list is Jim Stengel, who, as CMO, held the door open for purposeful innovation and welcomed me into his world as a friend. Fifteen years on, our friendship has grown, and that partnership has filled my life with opportunity and allowed me to live a dream. With his charisma, humanity and horsepower, he's done more to advance the global purpose movement than any other leader, and I'm grateful to have shared his journey.

In the early days of the purpose movement at P&G, I came in contact with two soul mates who helped make "purposology" a real discipline. Carolyn Hennessey and Dave Archer were genius collaborators in creating the processes and protocols that are the foundations of this book. Our whiteboard sessions together, filled with inspiration and laughter, rank among the most rewarding and life-changing experiences in my career.

I'm blessed to still call Carolyn one of my closest friends and collaborators.

Internally at P&G, there were several vanguards of purpose who pushed the organization forward and pushed my thinking forward as well. They included John Myers, Maria Brown, Carrie Barthel, Agnes Sangan and the leaders of brands like Pampers, Secret and Charmin. It was a tremendous honor and privilege to work with all of them.

We were also fueled by the contributions of Mario Simon, Benoit Garbe and their Millward-Brown Optimor colleagues; and P&G got tremendous energy and inspiration from Joey Reiman, CEO of BrightHouse, and Roy Spence, co-founder of GSD&M — two purpose luminaries whom I revere. They both powered my passion for a career in purpose and have inspired purpose seekers everywhere.

Under the leadership of CMO Marc Pritchard, our corporate purpose efforts were rolled into an initiative called "Brand Building 2020." The initiative team included Judith Azoulay, Heather Burgess, Katie Burns, Patricia DiMichele, Daniel Epstein, Dawn Haviland, Sharyl Michael, Andrea Schoff and Colleen Simpson. What a joy it was to do such game-changing work with such a power-packed group, and I still cherish the fun and friendship we shared. I'd like to extend special thanks to Marc Pritchard and Daniel Epstein for supporting me as I pursued my passion.

In the broader domain of branding, there are two great minds that I can never get enough of: my former P&G colleague Mary Nelson and Dr. Chris Allen, Professor Emeritus at the University of Cincinnati. Mary engaged with me on an early thought-piece that became this book, and she continues to inspire me — both in how she thinks about brands and in how she lives her life. Chris invited me into his classroom as a guest lecturer and then into his life as a friend. Over many years and beers, he shaped my thinking about marketing strategy and helped me crack many conceptual branding challenges. Many of the ideas in this book were brewed during my exhilarating discussions with Mary and Chris.

Since leaving P&G, my affiliation with The Jim Stengel Group has been an enormous gift. I'm deeply grateful to be connected to so much purposeful talent and energy and for the trust, mutual respect and affection we all share. During my time with JSG, I've spent the most "road hours" with Renée Dunn and Suzanne Tosolini. In the process of making lots of memories together, Renée has molded my thinking about internal purpose activation, and Suzanne has done the same on external activation. Their insightful perspectives are woven throughout this book. Both are like sisters to me, and I'm extremely thankful for their friendship and their contributions.

In the six years that I've been consulting, I've been blessed to work with some amazing clients. With each engagement, I've learned something powerful and made new friends. I can't name them all, but there are a few who were particularly instrumental in the beginning, providing follow-on opportunities that built my capability. They include Jeff Boutelle, Greg Economos, Andrea Theodore and Diane Ueberle. I'm immensely thankful for their trust and support.

As I finalized this book, there were a number of people who provided invaluable input. My heartfelt thanks go to Chris Allen, Suzanne Tosolini, Renée Dunn, Carolyn Hennessey, Sam Avivi, Lisa Hillenbrand and Jim Stengel for spending in-depth time with my manuscript. I'd also like to thank the team at Paramount Market Publishing, as well as Angela Wilcox for her graphics work. Finally, special thanks to my good friend Dave Knox for helping me get into publishing and for providing sage counsel.

The release of this book coincides with the twenty-fifth anniversary of my marriage, so I'd like to close this section by celebrating my wonderful wife Kristin. In our journey together, she is my rudder and my compass, and she puts the wind in my sails. I am blessed to have a partner with so much dignity, care, competence, composure and selfless commitment to the people she loves. She has supported and enabled my dreams and built my biggest one: our family. Our three sons — Nick, Ben and Will — are our pride and joy.

In writing this book, Kristin and the boys were my biggest source of encouragement and support, and Kristin spent countless hours providing input, research and counsel. For all that — and for all they are — my family has my deepest love and appreciation. They are my heartfelt devotion, the conviction that compels me.

APPENDIX A

Values Inventory

What appears below is a comprehensive survey of fundamental human values, bucketed by quadrant of the Point of View Compass. Note that the categorization of each word isn't precise. The lines between quadrants are blurred.

A: Achieve

Abundance	Competence	Efficiency	Glory
Accomplishment	Competition	Effort	Goals
Achievement	Competitiveness	Elevation	Grit
Action	Completion	Eminence	Guts
Activeness	Conquest	Endurance	Hard work
Adaptability	Courage	Enhancement	Heroism
Advancement	Craftiness	Energy	Impact
Affluence	Cunning	Exclusivity	Improvement
Aggressiveness	Daring	Expediency	Industry
Agility	Defiance	Expertise	Industriousness
Ambition	Determination	Extravagance	Influence
Aptitude	Development	Fearlessness	Initiative
Assertiveness	Dexterity	Ferocity	Intensity
Audacity	Distinction	Fierceness	Intrepidness
Authority	Doggedness	Fitness	Keenness
Boldness	Dominance	Fluency	Know-how
Bravery	Dreams	Forcefulness	Leadership
Capability	Drive	Fortitude	Majesty
Celebrity	Eagerness	Fulfillment	Mastery
Challenge	Effectiveness	Gallantry	Merit
Clout	Efficacy	Glamour	Nerve

A: Achieve

Performance	Recognition	Shrewdness	Utility
Perseverance	Relentlessness	Skill	Valor
Persistence	Resilience	Skillfulness	Victory
Popularity	Resolve	Speed	Vigor
Potency	Resourcefulness	Stamina	Wealth
Potential	Revolution	Steadfastness	Will
Power	Rigor	Strength	Willfulness
Prestige	Risk-taking	Success	Willingness
Pride	Self-assuredness	Superiority	Willpower
Proactivity	Self-determination	Supremacy	Winning
Proficiency	Self-improvement	Tenacity	Worthiness
Progress	Self-interest	Transformation	Vindication
Prosperity	Self-reliance	Triumph	
Rebellion	Self-sufficiency	Usefulness	

B: Belong

Acceptance	Communication	Faith	Humility
Accessibility	Communion	Faithfulness	Humor
Adoration	Community	Familiarity	Inclusion
Affability	Companionship	Family	Inclusiveness
Affection	Compassion	Fidelity	Inclusivity
Affiliation	Compromise	Flexibility	Interaction
Agreeableness	Conformity	Forgiveness	Interdependence
Altruism	Connection	Friendliness	Intimacy
Appreciation	Connectedness	Friendship	Involvement
Approachability	Consideration	Generosity	Kindness
Approval	Contribution	Genuineness	Love
Assimilation	Conviviality	Gentleness	Loyalty
Authenticity	Cooperation	Giving	Magnanimity
Belonging	Cordiality	Goodness	Marriage
Benevolence	Courteousness	Goodwill	Mercy
Camaraderie	Courtesy	Grace	Modesty
Care	Deference	Graciousness	Nature
Caring	Democracy	Gratefulness	Neighborliness
Charity	Devotion	Gratitude	Nostalgia
Charm	Devoutness	Happiness	Nurturance
Cheerfulness	Diplomacy	Harmony	Nurture
Civility	Encouragement	Helpfulness	Partnership
Closeness	Egalitarianism	Hospitality	Peace
Collaboration	Empathy	Humanity	Philanthropy
Comfort	Equality	Humanitarianism	Piety

B: Belong

Pleasantness
Reciprocity
Reconciliation
Relationships
Romance
Sacrifice
Selflessness
Self-sacrifice
Sensitivity

Sensuality
Sentimentality
Service
Sexuality
Sharing
Simplicity
Sociability
Solidarity
Spirituality

Support
Sympathy
Synergy
Teamwork
Tenderness
Thankfulness
Thoughtfulness
Togetherness
Tolerance

Tradition
Transparency
Trustworthiness
Unity
Universalism
Warmth

C: Control

Accountability
Accuracy
Assurance
Attractiveness
Austerity
Balance
Beauty
Calmness
Candidness
Candor
Carefulness
Caution
Certainty
Chasteness
Chastity
Cleanliness
Commitment
Composure
Connoisseurship
Conscientiousness
Conservation
Consistency
Constancy
Control
Convention
Correctness
Craftsmanship
Credibility
Decency
Decisiveness

Decorum
Dependability
Dignity
Diligence
Discernment
Discipline
Discretion
Duty
Elegance
Environmentalism
Equanimity
Esteem
Ethics
Etiquette
Exactitude
Exactness
Excellence
Exquisiteness
Fairness
Fame
Flawlessness
Focus
Formality
Frankness
Frugality
Gentility
Grace
Health
Hierarchy
Holiness

Honesty
Honor
Hygiene
Image
Impartiality
Incorruptibility
Integrity
Judgment
Judiciousness
Justice
Longevity
Maturity
Meticulousness
Moderation
Morality
Neatness
Obedience
Order
Orderliness
Organization
Ownership
Patience
Patriotism
Perfection
Planning
Poise
Polish
Politeness
Practicality
Pragmatism

Precision
Predictability
Preparedness
Preservation
Prevention
Privacy
Professionalism
Propriety
Protection
Protocol
Prudence
Punctuality
Purity
Quality
Rationality
Realism
Reason
Reasonability
Refinement
Regulation
Reliability
Reputation
Respect
Respectability
Responsibility
Restraint
Reverence
Rules
Sacredness
Safekeeping

C: Control

Safety	Sincerity	Structure	Truthfulness
Security	Sophistication	Sustainability	Uprightness
Self-control	Sportsmanship	Tact	Veracity
Self-discipline	Stability	Temperance	Well-being
Self-esteem	Standards	Thoroughness	Wholesomeness
Self-respect	Status	Thriftiness	
Sensibleness	Steadiness	Tidiness	
Serenity	Stewardship	Tranquility	

D: Discover & Experience

Adventure	Erudition	Inquiry	Passion
Amusement	Escape	Inquisitiveness	Perceptiveness
Art	Excitement	Insightfulness	Perkiness
Artistry	Experience	Inspiration	Play
Astuteness	Experimentation	Intellect	Playfulness
Autonomy	Exploration	Intelligence	Pleasure
Awe	Expression	Introspection	Possibility
Bliss	Expressiveness	Intuition	Rapture
Brilliance	Exuberance	Intuitiveness	Recreation
Buoyancy	Fascination	Invention	Relaxation
Celebration	Fantasy	Inventiveness	Revelry
Change	Free will	Invigoration	Sagacity
Choice	Freedom	Joie de vivre	Scholarship
Clarity	Free-spiritedness	Joy	Self-direction
Cleverness	Fun	Knowledge	Self-expression
Consciousness	Genius	Learning	Sovereignty
Contemplation	Gladness	Leisure	Spontaneity
Contentment	Glee	Liberation	Stimulation
Creativity	Gratification	Liberty	Surprise
Curiosity	Growth	Liveliness	Transcendence
Delight	Hedonism	Merriment	Truth
Discovery	Hopefulness	Mindfulness	Understanding
Diversity	Idealism	Nonconformity	Uniqueness
Dynamism	Imagination	Novelty	Vitality
Ease	Independence	Open-mindedness	Vivaciousness
Education	Individualism	Openness	Vivacity
Enjoyment	Individuality	Opportunity	Wit
Enlightenment	Indulgence	Optimism	Wittiness
Entertainment	Ingenuity	Originality	Wonder
Enthusiasm	Innocence	Outlandishness	Youthfulness
Entrepreneurship	Innovation	Outrageousness	Zeal

APPENDIX B
Sample Purpose Statements

The following are actual purpose statements as publicly presented at the time of writing. They are judged to meet most, if not all, of the criteria outlined in Chapter 2. To aid the usability of the list, the statements are organized by business type.

Consumer Products

Barbie	To inspire and nurture the limitless possibilities of girls
Beech-Nut	To help every mom and dad share the lifelong joy of real food with their babies
Betty Crocker	To help people 'make home'
Burt's Bees	To reconnect people to the wisdom, power and beauty of nature
Carhartt	To serve and protect hardworking people
Charmin	To help people 'enjoy the go'
Crayola	To inspire creatively alive kids
Dove	To help more women feel beautiful every day

Dulux	To add colour to people's lives
Excedrin	To set minds free
Graco	To cradle those who cradle them
Harley-Davidson	To fulfill dreams of personal freedom
Honey Maid	To nourish togetherness
Lean Cuisine	To feed the greatness of every woman
LEGO	To inspire and develop the builders of tomorrow
Life is Good	To spread the power of optimism
MegaFood	To nourish a world in nutritional crisis
Meguiar's	To fuel the passion people have for their cars
MET-Rx	To fuel athletes to master their destiny
Nike	To bring inspiration and innovation to every athlete
Nintendo	To bring entertainment, delight and joy to people's lives
Nutro	To help dogs live long and thrive
Pampers	To care for all babies' happy, healthy development
Plum Organics	To nourish little ones with the very best food from the very first bite
Red Bull	To uplift mind and body
Secret	To help women take on each day as fearlessly as they can
Special K	To help every woman live life at full strength

Stanfield's Underwear	To support men
Stella Artois	To bring out the discerning gentleman in all of us
Symantec	To empower people to protect their digital rights
Tesla	To accelerate the world's transition to sustainable energy
Total	To help people realize the potential that comes with age
Wheaties	To fuel the champion within

Consumer Retail / Service

Airbnb	To create a world where everyone can 'belong anywhere'
American Family Insurance	To inspire, protect and restore dreams
Cincinnati Ballet	To move people profoundly and joyfully
Curves	To strengthen women
CVS	To help people on their path to better health
Development Bank of Singapore (DBS Bank)	To make banking joyful
Disney	To bring happiness to millions
Dunkin' Donuts	To keep America running
Facebook	To give people the power to build community and bring the world closer together
Geek Squad	To help ordinary people do extraordinary things with technology
Google	To organize the world's information and make it universally accessible and useful

H&M	To make sustainable fashion choices available, attractive, and affordable to as many people as possible
IKEA	To create a better everyday life for the many people
Kroger	To feed the human spirit
Lane Bryant	To change the way women see themselves in the world and change the way the world sees them
Lowe's	To help people love where they live
MGM Resorts	To blow the mind of all mankind
The New York Times	To help people understand the world
Patagonia	To save our home planet
Pinterest	To help people discover things they love and inspire them to do those things
REI	To inspire, educate and outfit people for a lifetime of outdoor adventure and stewardship
Seasons 52	To inspire people to enjoy a better way to eat
Southwest	To connect people to what's important in their lives
Starbucks	To inspire and nurture the human spirit — one person, one cup, one neighborhood at a time
SunTrust Bank	To light the way to financial well-being
Twitter	To give everyone the power to create and share ideas and information instantly, without barriers
Walmart	To help people save money and live better

B2B / Professional Services

DTE Energy	To serve with our energy, the lifeblood of communities and the engine of progress
EY	To build a better work world

Harvard Business Review	To improve the practice of management in a changing world
LPK	To give brands the creativity, vision and courage to be extraordinary
McKinsey	To help leading corporations and governments be more successful
Medtronic	To help real people overcome pain and disability to lead more normal, happy lives
Motorola Solutions	To help people be their best in moments that matter
Old Dominion	To help the world keep promises
TED	To spread ideas
We Work	To create a world where people work to make a life, not just a living
Zurich	To help people understand and protect themselves from risk

Non-Profits / Government

AARP	To champion positive social change that will enhance the quality of life for all as we age
American Legacy Foundation	To build a world where young people reject tobacco and anyone can quit
American Red Cross	To enable Americans to perform extraordinary acts in the face of emergencies
Change.org	To empower people everywhere to create the change they want to see
Orange County (California) Court System	To unclog the wheels of justice
Salvation Army	To make citizens of the rejected
The Mission Continues	To rehabilitate and reintegrate into society wounded and disabled war veterans
UNICEF	To help every child worldwide reach their full potential

| Wharton Center at Michigan State University | To inspire the mind and move the soul |

Multi-Brand Corporations

3M	To solve unsolved problems innovatively
General Mills	To nourish lives
J.M. Smucker	To bring families together to share memorable meals and moments
L'Oreal	To empower women to leave their mark on their world
Pharmavite	To bring the gift of health to life
Unilever	To make sustainable living commonplace

APPENDIX C

Sample Operating Values

The following are actual statements of operating values as publicly presented at the time of writing. They generally follow the guidelines outlined in Chapter 2.

Barclay's	
Respect	We respect and value those we work with, and the contribution that they make.
Integrity	We act fairly, ethically and openly in all we do.
Service	We put our clients and customers at the center of what we do.
Excellence	We use our energy, skills and resources to deliver the best, sustainable results.
Stewardship	We are passionate about leaving things better than we found them.

IDEO	
Be optimistic	Believing that something is possible will somehow make it so.
Collaborate	The most powerful asset we have in our arsenal is the word "we."

Embrace ambiguity	Get comfortable with uncomfortable-ness.
Learn from failure	Ask for forgiveness, not permission.
Make others successful	Going out of your way to help others succeed is the secret sauce.
Take ownership	The unwritten social contract here: individual ownership supports collective responsibility. Own that.
Talk less, do more	Nothing is a bigger buzz-kill than over-intellectualizing. Design is about rolling up your sleeves and making something.

Innocent

Be natural	Not just our products, but being natural in how we treat each other and how we speak to everyone — colleagues, drinkers, customers, suppliers, etc. It also means being ourselves, and the best version of it.
Be entrepreneurial	Innocent began as a small, entrepreneurial company, and although we've grown a lot since, we do keep our entrepreneurial mindset. We aren't afraid to do things differently, and we've never given up on a good opportunity.
Be responsible	We keep our promises, are mindful of our impact on our community and our environment, and always try to leave things a little bit better than we found them.
Be commercial	We wouldn't be here if we didn't keep our eyes on the numbers at all times. Ultimately we want to deliver growth for us and our customers too.
Be generous	This means giving honest feedback to one another, helping each other out, taking time to say thank you, and where we can, donating our resources or money to those who need it more than us. It's that simple.

The Motley Fool

Collaborate	Do great things together.
Innovate	Search for a better solution. Then top it!
Fun	Revel in your work.
Honest	Make us proud.

Competitive	Play fair, play hard, play to win.
Motley	Make Foolishness your own.

Netflix

Judgment	Making wise decisions; identify root causes; think strategically
Communication	Listen well; concise speech; respectful
Impact	Amazing amounts of important work; consistently strong performance; focus on results, not process; bias to action, not analysis
Curiosity	Learn rapidly; seek to understand; broad knowledge
Innovation	Re-conceptualize issues to discover practical solutions; challenge prevailing assumptions; create new ideas that prove useful
Courage	Say what you think; make tough decisions; take smart risks; question actions inconsistent with their values
Passion	Inspire others with excellence; care intensely about company success; celebrate wins; tenacious
Honesty	Candor and directness; non-political; quick to admit mistakes
Selflessness	Seek what is best for Netflix; egoless when searching for best ideas; help colleagues; share info openly and proactively

Novartis

Innovation	By experimenting and delivering solutions
Quality	By taking pride in doing ordinary things extraordinarily well
Collaboration	By championing high performing teams with diversity and inclusion
Performance	By prioritizing and making things happen with urgency
Courage	By speaking up, giving and receiving feedback
Integrity	By advocating and applying high ethical standards every day

Terakeet	
Integrity	Upholding the highest standards of trust and character throughout the organization.
Sustainable Value	Creating long-term return on investment for customers.
Entrepreneurship	Empowering every individual, no matter their role, with the ability to control the destiny of the company.
Invention	Continuing the legacy of actualizing the company's first-to-market ideas and strategies.
Rapid Response	Listening to customers and providing the attention of an ambitious startup firm no matter how large we grow.

Sample Manifestos

The following is a selection of manifestos recently or currently used in market.

Carhartt

Carhartt is for folks who, at the end of a long, hard day, still make time to teach their kids how to swing a baseball bat, draw plans for a tree house, or get after it in the great outdoors. Product engineered to go from field to field, job to job, helping hardworking men and women maximize every beautiful minute of every beautiful day – and sometimes even the not so beautiful moments too. That's our job. Make the very best product, for the very best people.

Source: Catalog

Diesel

Like balloons, we are filled with hopes and dreams, but over time a single sentence creeps into our lives – Don't be stupid. It's the crusher of possibility. It's the world's greatest deflator. The world is full of smart people doing all kinds of smart things. That's smart. Well, we're with stupid. Stupid is the relentless pursuit of a regret-free life. Smart may have the brains, but stupid has the balls. Smart recognizes things for how they are. Stupid sees things for how they could be. Smart critiques. Stupid creates. The fact is, if we didn't have stupid thoughts, we'd have no interesting thoughts at all. Smart may have the plans . . . but stupid has the stories. Smart may have the authority, but stupid has one hell of a hangover. It's not smart to take risks, it's stupid. To be stupid is to be brave. Stupid isn't afraid to fail. Stupid knows there are worse things than failure. Like not even trying. Smart had one good idea and that idea was stupid. You can't outsmart stupid. So don't even try. Remember, only stupid can be truly brilliant. So, be stupid!

Source: https://www.youtube.com/watch?v=Y4h8uOUConE

Johnson's Baby

For nearly 125 years Johnson's mission has been to create the gentlest baby products in the world. Products so mild, they can be used for every age and stage of a baby's life.

That's our standard of gentle. But gentle isn't only in our bottles, it is also in our heart.

At Johnson's, we believe in the immense, transformative power of gentle in the world. Of being gentle with our children, and with their dreams and ambitions. Gentle with each other. Gentle with the earth. Gentle with our words and thoughts and actions. Gentle means safe. Gentle means pure. Gentle means confident. Gentle means happy.

That's why everything we make, everything we do and everything we stand for is as gentle as you want the world to be.

Source: Brand website

Kaiser Permanente

We stand for broccoli. For Pilates. And dental floss. We believe in the treadmill and its siblings StairMaster and elliptical. In SPF 30 we trust. We stand for seat belts and stopping HIV. And we believe fruit makes a wonderful dessert. We have faith in optimism. In laughter as medicine as well as penicillin. And we pledge allegiance to one nation, indivisible, with resistance and cardio for all. We believe in physical therapy, psychotherapy, even music as therapy. All hail cold turkey, the gum, and the patch. We're anti-addiction. Pro-antioxidant. And have never met a vegetable we didn't like. We believe there is art to medicine as well as science. And we believe health isn't an industry, it's a cause. We are Kaiser Permanente and we stand for health. May you live long and thrive.

Source: http://www.520collective.org/story-kaiser-permanente/

Life is Good

Life is not perfect. Life is not easy. Life is good.

We see it when we believe it. Each one of us has a choice: to focus our energy on obstacles or opportunities. To fixate on our problems, or focus on solutions. We can harp on what's wrong with the world (see most news media), or we can cultivate what's right with the world. What we focus on grows.

That's why the Life is Good community shares one simple, unifying mission: to spread the power of optimism.

Optimism is not irrational cheerfulness or "blind" positivity. It's a pragmatic strategy for approaching life. Optimism empowers us to explore the world with open arms and an eye toward solutions, progress, and growth. It also makes life a hell of a lot more fun.

Optimism also enables us to access the ten most important tools we have for living a happy and fulfilling life. We call them the Life is Good Superpowers. But unlike X-ray vision, bullet speed, or Herculean strength, they are accessible to us all. The Life is Good Superpowers can help you overcome obstacles, drive forward with greater purpose, and enjoy the ride of life.

Source: Company website

Marucci

Commitment is more than a word.

It's stronger than a pledge and deeper than a promise.

It's something you embody and something you earn.

It takes consistency, passion, heart, and confidence.

Commitment is unbreakable. It's a steadfast conviction vetted by adversity and affirmed by success. It instills a mental toughness that silences critics, eliminates doubt, and inspires confidence.

Commitment is a responsibility. It's the pledge that drives you and lights a fire within. It's an obligation you have to your family, your home, your team, and yourself. It's rooted in pride, inspired by purpose, and fueled by passion.

Commitment is ongoing. It's a relentless pursuit of excellence that requires a willingness to give your all to the game and your team. It's defined by determination, assessed by attitude, and measured by heart.

Consistency in preparation translates to consistency on the field. It requires a pledge to the process and a daily dedication to your routine.

Source: Company website

Method

As people against dirty,

We look at the world through bright-green colored glasses.

We see ingredients that come from plants, not chemical plants.

We see that guinea pigs are never used as guinea pigs.

We're entranced by shiny objects like clean dinner plates, floors you could eat off of, nobel peace prizes, and tasteful public sculptures.

We're an e.o.m.e.d. (equal opportunity movement for

environment and design). Method is our way of keeping the movement, well, moving.

We make role models in bottles.

We're the kind of people who've figured out that once you clean your home, a mess of other problems seem to disappear too.

We always see the aroma pill as half full, and assume everyone we meet smells like fresh-cut grass or a similar yummy nothing-but-good fragrance.

We exercise by running through the legs of the giant.

And while we love a freshly detoxed home, we think perfect is boring, and weirdliness is next to godliness.

It's "everybody into the pool!" (we believe in spontaneous bursts of enthusiasm.)

We also believe in making products safe for every surface, especially earth's.

We consider mistakes little messes we can learn from—nothing that can't be cleaned up and made better.

We embrace the golden ylang-ylang rule: do unto your home as you would do unto you. (your shower doesn't want to have morning breath any more than you do.)

We believe above all else that dirty, in all its slime, smoggy, toxic, disgusting incarnations is public enemy number one.

Good always prevails over stinky.

Source: "The Method Method" by Eric Ryan and Adam Lowry

Yeti

In the wild, we're never the ones in charge. We only know ourselves and our gear and set out to let the pursuit teach us a thing or two.

But out there, what might take us down can instead build us up. And there's only one way to find out.

We go full-bore into uncharted territory, willing to trust a stranger on belay, ignoring instincts that say "shark," and finding out it's possible to rope, fish, and hunt — all in one day.

There's no better way to do it. That's why everything we make is built for the wild — because there's nowhere we'd rather be.

Source: Spring-Summer 2018 catalog

Endnotes

Introduction

1. EY Beacon Institute. "The state of the debate of purpose in business." 2016.

2. Collins, James C. and Jerry I. Porras. *Built to Last* (New York: Harper Business, 1994) p. 4.

3. Sisodia, Raj, Jag Sheth and David B. Wolfe. *Firms of Endearment* (Upper Saddle River, New Jersey: Wharton School Publishing, 2007) p. 16.

4. Stengel, Jim. *Grow* (New York: Crown Business, 2011) p. 37.

5. Kantar Vermeer, Esomar, ARF, LinkedIn and Korn Ferry. "Driving Customer-Centric Growth," Insights2020, 2014.

6. Gartenberg, Claudine, Andrea Prat, and George Serafeim. "Corporate Purpose and Financial Performance." Harvard Business School Working Paper, №17–023, September 2016.

7. Interbrand. "2017 Best Global Brands: Growth from the inside out." 2017. https://www.interbrand.com/best-brands/best-global-brands/2017/articles/growth-from-the-inside-out/.

8. Strauss, Karsten. "The 10 Companies With the Best CSR Reputations In 2017, *Forbes*. September 13, 2017. https://www.forbes.com/sites/karstenstrauss/2017/09/13/the-10-companies-with-the-best-csr-reputations-in-2017/#7fd990e9546b.

9. Mainwaring, Simon. "How Lego Rebuilt Itself As a Purposeful and Sustainable Brand," *Forbes*. August 11, 2016. https://www.forbes.com/sites/simonmainwaring/2016/08/11/how-lego-rebuilt-itself-as-a-purposeful-and-sustainable-brand/#2e6f46476f3c.

10. Deloitte. "Culture of Purpose – Building business confidence; driving growth: 2014 core beliefs & culture survey," 2014.

11. PwC. "Putting Purpose to Work: A Study of Purpose in the Workplace," June 2016.

12. Deloitte. "Culture of Purpose – Building business confidence; driving growth: 2014 core beliefs & culture survey," 2014.

13. Mannion, Lee. "Young entrepreneurs motivated by purpose, not just profit," Reuters. June 11, 2018. https://www.reuters.com/article/us-global-business-ethics/young-entrepreneurs-motivated-by-purpose-not-just-profit-idUSKBN1J8003.

14. Cone Communications. "2016 Cone Communications Employee Engagement Survey." https://www.conecomm.com/research-blog/2016-employee-engagement-study.

15. Kotler, Philip, Hermawan Kartajaya and Iwan Setiawan. *Marketing 3.0* (Hoboken, New Jersey: John Wiley & Sons, 2010) p. 126.

16. Walshe, Peter. "10 traits of megabrands," *Admap*. February 2016. http://zenithinfostation.my/wp-content/uploads/2016/05/test-1.pdf.

17. Edelman Earned Brand. "Brands Take a Stand," October 2018. https://www.edelman.com/sites/default/files/2018-10/2018_Edelman_Earned_Brand_Global_Report.pdf?utm_source=website&utm_campaign=2018_edelman_earned_brand_global_report_download.

18. Harvard Business Review Analytical Services. "The Business Case for Purpose," 2015.

19. Sweeney, Erica. "Study: Brands with a purpose grow 2X faster than others," Marketing Dive. April 19, 2018. https://www.marketingdive.com/news/study-brands-with-a-purpose-grow-2x-faster-than-others/521693/.

20. SNL, "Pitch Meeting," February 12, 2017. https://www.youtube.com/watch?v=imUigBNF-TE.

Part 1 | Chapter 1

1. National Park Service website. "Seventh Debate: Alton, Illinois." https://www.nps.gov/liho/learn/historyculture/debate7.htm.

2. Griessman, Gene. *The Words Lincoln Lived By* (New York: Fireside, 1997) p. 100.

3. Ibid., p. 7.

4. Kerpen, Dave. "Why Passion Matters, According To 15 of the World's Most Inspiring People," *Huffington Post*. April 2, 2014. https://www.huffingtonpost.com/2014/04/02/inspiring-quotes-passion_n_5077853.html.

5. Whitten, Sarah. "Life is Good's $100 million ad-free global success story," CNBC. May 29, 2015. https://www.cnbc.com/2015/05/19/life-is-good-for-bert-and-john-jacobs.html.

6. St. Jude Children's Research Hospital website. "Our Unique Operating Model." https://www.stjude.org/about-st-jude/unique-operating-model.html.

7. YCharts website. "Nike Inc Market Cap." https://ycharts.com/companies/NKE/market_cap.

8. The Fitco Training Portal website. "Nike." https://trainingatthefitco.wordpress.com/2014/09/12/nike/.

9. O'Brien, Sara Ashley. "Here's What's Wrong with Uber — According to Uber," CNN Business. June 13, 2017. https://money.cnn.com/2017/06/13/technology/business/uber-workplace-culture-report/index.html.

10. Yurieff, Kaya. "Lyft is now worth twice what it was last year," *CNN Business.* June 27, 2018. http://money.cnn.com/2018/06/27/technology/lyft-funding-round/index.html.

11. Airbnb. "Airbnb Introduces the Bélo: The Story of a Symbol of Belonging." July 24, 2014. https://www.youtube.com/watch?v=nMITXMrrVQU.

12. Airbnb website. "Diversity." https://www.airbnb.com/diversity.

13. Clune, Bronwen. "How Airbnb is Building Its Culture Through Belonging," Culture Amp blog. https://blog.cultureamp.com/how-airbnb-is-building-its-culture-through-belonging.

14. Darrow, Barb. Interview with Brian Chesky. "Airbnb's CEO Talks about Trump's Travel Ban," *Fortune.* February 10, 2017. http://fortune.com/2017/02/10/airbnb-ceo-travel-ban-super-bowl-ad/.

15. Cohan, Roger. "Airbnb is the New NATO," *The New York Times.* August 3, 2018. https://www.nytimes.com/2018/08/03/opinion/airbnb-is-the-new-nato.html.

16. Bort, Julie. "Airbnb made $93 million in profit on $2.6 billion in revenue, but an internal clash sent the CFO out the door," *Business Insider.* February 6, 2018. https://www.businessinsider.com/airbnb-profit-revenue-2018-2.

17. Simmons, John. *The Starbucks Story* (Marshall Cavendish Business, 2012) p. 69.

18. Wiener-Bronner, Danielle. "Starbucks achieves pay equity in the United States," CNN Business. March 21, 2018. https://money.cnn.com/2018/03/21/news/companies/starbucks-pay-equity/index.html.

19. Starbucks website. "Ethical Sourcing: Coffee." https://www.starbucks.com/responsibility/sourcing/coffee.

20. Lincoln, Keith and Lars Thomassen. *How to Succeed at Retail* (Kogan Page, 2009) p. 153.

21. Schultz, Howard. Interview by Oprah Winfrey. "Super Soul Sunday—The Coffee Culture Howard Schultz Wanted to Bring to America." Season 4, Episode 435. December 8, 2013. http://www.oprah.com/own-super-soul-sunday/the-coffee-culture-howard-schultz-wanted-to-bring-to-America-video.

22. Schultz, Howard with Joanne Gordon. *Onward* (New York: Rodale, 2001) p. 117.

23. Closson, Clayton. "The Pegasus Grill – Gourmet Cooking for the Front Line," WhatsTheDiff blog. August 27, 2007. Website no longer available.

24. Pontefract, Dan. *The Purpose Effect* (Vancouver: Figure.1, 2016) p. 144.

25. Ibid., p.143.

26. Riley, Tonya. "What It Means to Be a Working-Class Clothing Brand in America Today," *Esquire*. July 14, 2017. https://www.esquire.com/style/mens-fashion/a56175/carhartt-american-workwear/.

27. Brack, Charles. "Conservative Left Brain, Liberal Right Brain." Neuropolitics. March 2005. http://neuropolitics.org/Conservative-Left-Brain-Liberal-Right-Brain.htm.

28. Ibid.

29. Jacobs, Laura. "From Hermès to Eternity," *Vanity Fair.* September 2007. p. 378.

30. Ibid., p. 383.

Chapter 2

1. Schultz, Howard with Joanne Gordon. *Onward* (New York: Rodale, 2001) p. 96.

2. Warren, Rick. *The Purpose-Driven Life* (Grand Rapids, Michigan: Zondervan, 2002) p. 32.

3. Kamprad, Ingvar. *The Testament of a Furniture Dealer.* Inter IKEA Systems B.V. 2007. p. 24.

4. Muoio, Anna. "The Secrets of Their Success – and Yours," *Fast Company*. June 30, 1997. https://www.fastcompany.com/29098/secrets-their-success-and-yours.

5. GoodReads website. https://www.goodreads.com/quotes/179393-a-belief-system-is-nothing-more-than-a-thought-you-ve.

6. Reiman, Joey. *The Story of Purpose* (Hoboken, New Jersey: John Wiley & Sons, Inc., 2013) p. 43.

7. Ready, Lauren, interview with Daniel Lubetzky. "The amazing story behind that KIND bar you're eating," *USA Today*. March 30, 2015.

https://www.usatoday.com/story/news/2015/03/30/inspiration-nation-daniel-lubetzky-kind/70676954/.

8. Sachs, MaryLee. "Does Brand Purpose Drive Great Creative?," *Forbes*. September 5, 2017. https://www.forbes.com/sites/maryleesachs/2017/09/05/does-brand-purpose-drive-great-creative/#1ce842b21cc1.

Part 2 | Chapter 3

1. Pink, Daniel H. *Drive* (New York: Riverhead Books, 2009) p. 133.

2. PwC. "Putting Purpose to Work: A Study of Purpose in the Workplace," June 2016.

3. IBM Corporation and Globoforce Limited. "The Employee Experience Index," September 2016.

4. The Energy Project and *Harvard Business Review*. "The Human Era @ Work: Findings from The Energy Project and Harvard Business Review," 2014. https://uli.org/wp-content/uploads/ULI-Documents/The-Human-Era-at-Work.pdf.

5. Kotter, John P. and James L. Heskett. *Corporate Culture and Performance* (Free Press, 2011).

6. Spencer Stuart. "Spencer Stuart CMO Summit." Conference invitation. March 11, 2015.

7. "Small Team Strategies are the Key to New Success," Dr. David Powers blog. September 1, 2017. https://redteamgoals.com/tag/peter-drucker/.

8. Schaefer, Wolfgang and JP Kuehlwein. *Rethinking Prestige Branding* (London: Kogan Page, 2015) p. 48.

9. Chouinard, Yvon. *Let My People Go Surfing* (New York: Penguin Books, 2005) p. 31.

10. Collins, James C. and Jerry I. Porras. *Built to Last* (New York: Harper Business, 1994) p. 8.

11. "Joy of Patagonia," *The Hub*. November/December 2014. p. 28.

12. "The Odd Couple of French Winemaking." March 15, 2008. https://www.youtube.com/watch?v=pV0QIpp3U9k.

13. Altman, Jonas. "Are Culture and Leadership Two Sides of the Same Coin? It Depends," *Inc*. October 31, 2017. https://www.inc.com/jonas-altman/culture-leadership-are-two-sides-of-same-coin-or-are-they.html.

14. "IBM's John Kennedy focuses on more interconnected, intelligent world," *AdAge*. February 4, 2013. https://adage.com/article/btob/ibm-s-john-kennedy-focuses-interconnected-intelligent-world/288781/.

15. Taylor, Bill. "Brand is Culture, Culture is Brand," *Harvard Business*

Review. September 27, 2010. https://hbr.org/2010/09/brand-is-culture-culture-is-br.

16. Pfau, Bruce N. "How an Accounting Firm Convinced Its Employees They Could Change the World," *Harvard Business Review.* October 6, 2015. https://hbr.org/2015/10/how-an-accounting-firm-convinced-its-employees-they-could-change-the-world.

17. Meek, Andy. "Google's Head of HR Shares His Hiring Secrets," *Fast Company.* April 6, 2015. https://www.fastcompany.com/3044606/googles-head-of-hr-shares-his-hiring-secrets.

18. Yohn, Denise Lee. *Fusion* (Boston: Nicholas Brealey Publishing, 2018) p. 82.

19. Smith, Emily Esfahani and Jennifer Aaker. "Millennial Searchers," *New York Times.* November 30, 2013. https://www.nytimes.com/2013/12/01/opinion/sunday/millennial-searchers.html.

20. Pearlman, Russell. "Profit vs. Purpose: The Duel Begins," Korn Ferry Institute. May 15, 2018. https://www.kornferry.com/institute/the-duel-begins.

21. Aaker, David. *Aaker on Branding* (New York: Morgan James Publishing, 2014) p. 128.

22. Yohn, Denise Lee. *Fusion* (Boston: Nicholas Brealey Publishing, 2018) p. xx.

23. Cone Communications. "2017 Cone Gen Z CSR Study: How to Speak Z." https://www.conecomm.com/research-blog/2017-genz-csr-study.

24. Eng, Dinah. "Does Joy Help You Sell?," *Fortune.* January 1, 2015, p. 30.

25. Yohn, Denise Lee. *Fusion* (Boston: Nicholas Brealey Publishing, 2018) p. 119.

26. Quinn, Robert E. and Anjan V. Thakor. "Creating a Purpose-Driven Organization," *Harvard Business Review,* July-August 2018.

27. Walmart website. "Our History." http://corporate.walmart.com/our-story/our-history.

28. Yohn, Denise Lee. *Fusion* (Boston: Nicholas Brealey Publishing, 2018) p. 125.

29. Michelli, Joseph A. *The New Gold Standard* (New York: McGraw-Hill, 2008) pp. 37-39 and 188.

30. Ryan, Eric and Adam Lowry. *The Method Method* (New York: Portfolio, 2011) pp. 53-55 and 151.

31. Gelles, David. "Merck C.E.O. Ken Frazier on Death Row Cases and the Corporate Soul," *The New York Times.* March 9, 2018. https://www.nytimes.com/2018/03/09/business/merck-ceo-ken-frazier-on-death-row-cases-and-the-corporate-soul.html.

32. Yohn, Denise Lee. *Fusion* (Boston: Nicholas Brealey Publishing, 2018) p. 147.

33. Lehrer, Jonah. "The Psychology of Architecture," *Wired.* April 14, 2011. https://www.wired.com/2011/04/the-psychology-of-architecture/.

34. Yohn, Denise Lee. *Fusion* (Boston: Nicholas Brealey Publishing, 2018) p. 97.

35. Nusca, Andrew. "84 Activision Blizzard," *Fortune.* March 1, 2018. pp. 92-94.

36. Tjan, Anthony K. "6 Rules for Building and Scaling Company Culture," *Harvard Business Review.* March 23, 2015. https://hbr.org/2015/03/6-rules-for-building-and-scaling-company-culture.

37. GoodReads website. https://www.goodreads.com/quotes/423173-a-leader-is-one-who-knows-the-way-goes-the.

38. Sellers, Patricia. "How great marketers tell stories," Part 5 of a series by Jim Stengel with Chris Allen. *Fortune.* April 18, 2014.

39. Interview with Jim Stengel, September 11, 2009.

40. GoodReads website. https://www.goodreads.com/quotes/55597-example-is-not-the-main-thing-in-influencing-others-it.

41. Kowitt, Beth. "It's IKEA's World," *Fortune.* March 15, 2015. p. 169.

42. "Crowe Horwath. Profile 2018 | Best Companies to Work For," Ad Section, *Fortune.* March 1, 2018.

43. PwC. "Putting Purpose to Work: A Study of Purpose in the Workplace," June 2016.

44. Barnes, Julian E. "P.&G. Said to Agree to Pay Unilever $10 Million in Spying Case," *The New York Times.* September 7, 2001. https://www.nytimes.com/2001/09/07/business/p-g-said-to-agree-to-pay-unilever-10-million-in-spying-case.html.

45. Ready, Lauren, interview with Daniel Lubetzky. "The amazing story behind that KIND bar you're eating," *USA Today.* March 30, 2015.

Chapter 4

1. Collins, James C. and Jerry I. Porras. *Built to Last* (New York: Harper Business, 1994) p. 56.

2. Deloitte. "Culture of Purpose – Building business confidence; driving growth: 2014 core beliefs & culture survey," 2014.

3. Oprah website. "Every Person Has a Purpose." http://www.oprah.com/spirit/how-oprah-winfrey-found-her-purpose.

4. Allen, Scott. "Oprah Winfrey's and Her Business Ventures," *The*

Balance Small Business. July 22, 2018. https://www.thebalancesmb.
com/oprah-winfrey-entrepreneur-1200951.

5. "Oprah Winfrey on Career, Life, and Leadership." Stanford Graduate
School of Business. April 28, 2014. https://www.youtube.com/
watch?v=6DlrqeWrczs&feature=youtu.behttps%3A%2F%2F

6. Mannion, Lee. "Young entrepreneurs motivated by purpose, not just
profit," Reuters. June 11, 2018. https://www.reuters.com/article/
us-global-business-ethics/young-entrepreneurs-motivated-by-
purpose-not-just-profit-idUSKBN1J8003.

7. WARC website. "Under Armour keeps brand 'fluid.'" April 14, 2016.
https://www.warc.com/newsandopinion/news/under_armour_keeps_
brand_fluid/36571.

8. High, Peter. "Under Armour Is Now The Largest Digital Health And
Fitness Company On Earth," *Forbes.* September 18, 2017. https://
www.forbes.com/sites/peterhigh/2017/09/18/under-armour-
is-now-the-largest-digital-health-and-fitness-company-on-
earth/#4386f8915dfc.

9. Mars website. "Mars Petcare." http://www.mars.com/global/brands/
petcare.

10. Moon, Youngme. *Different: Escaping the Competitive Herd* (Crown
Business, 2011) p. 248.

11. Red Bull website. "The Company Behind the Can." http://
energydrink-us.redbull.com/en/company.

12. "Mr Red Bull: Dietrich Mateschitz," *The Local.* June 13, 2014.
https://www.thelocal.at/20140613/mr-red-bull-dietrich-mateschitz.

13. Zorfas, Alan and Daniel Leemon. "An Emotional Connection Matters
More Than Customer Satisfaction," *Harvard Business Review.* August
29, 2016. https://hbr.org/2016/08/an-emotional-connection-matters-
more-than-customer-satisfaction.

14. Travis, Daryl. *Emotional Branding* (Crown Business, 2000).

15. SAS website. "A lesson in customer service from Chick-fil-A
President Dan Cathy." https://www.sas.com/en_us/insights/articles/
marketing/a-lesson-in-customer-service-from-chick-fil-a.html.

16. Davis, Scott. "Chick-fil-A's Raving Fans' Growth Strategy,"
Forbes. December 13, 2013. https://www.forbes.com/sites/
scottdavis/2013/12/16/chick-fil-as-raving-fans-growth-strategy/
#72ab06181fb5.

17. Seth, Gauri. "Chick-fil-A Case Study: Service Training is Key to
Staying in Business," LinkedIn. October 10, 2016. https://www.
linkedin.com/pulse/chick-fil-a-case-study-why-customer-service-
training-key-gauri-seth/.

18. Fruit, Josh. Interview with Paul Cobban. "DBS Bank's Agile Transformation to Make Banking Joyful," AgileAmped. February 23, 2017. https://www.youtube.com/watch?v=l7TifhEt0yE.

19. Craig, Nick. *Leading from Purpose* (New York: Hachette Books, 2018) p. 244.

20. Baskin, Jonathan Salem. "Can DBS Make Banking Joyful?," *Forbes*. December 21, 2015. https://www.forbes.com/sites/jonathansalembaskin/2015/12/21/can-dbs-make-banking-joyful/#e8a679c9888e.

21. "A record first half." DBS. https://www.dbs.com/iwov-resources/pdf/investor/financial-performance/2018/2Q18_presentation_slides.pdf.

Chapter 5

1. Edelman Earned Brand. "Brands Take a Stand," October 2018. https://www.edelman.com/sites/default/files/2018-10/2018_Edelman_Earned_Brand_Global_Report.pdf?utm_source=website&utm_campaign=2018_edelman_earned_brand_global_report_download.

2. Global Strategy Group press release. "New study finds corporations have a responsibility to lead on issues of the day, right behind the President and US Congress." December 7, 2016. https://www.globalstrategygroup.com/wp-content/uploads/2016/12/Press-Release-1.pdf.

3. Cone Communications. "2016 Cone Communications Employee Engagement Survey." https://www.conecomm.com/research-blog/2016-employee-engagement-study.

4. BlackRock website. "A Sense of Purpose." https://www.blackrock.com/corporate/investor-relations/larry-fink-ceo-letter.

5. Montgomery, David Bruce and Catherine A. Ramus. "Corporate Social Responsibility Reputation Effects on MBA Job Choice," Stanford Business, Working Paper No. 1805, 2003.

6. Cone press release. "Three-Quarters of Millennials Would Take a Pay Cut to Work for a Socially Responsible Company, According to the Research from Cone Communications." November 2, 2016. http://www.conecomm.com/news-blog/2016-cone-communications-millennial-employee-engagement-study-press-release.

7. Kotler, Philip, Hermawan Kartajaya and Iwan Setiawan. *Marketing 3.0* (Hoboken, New Jersey: John Wiley & Sons, 2010) p. 126.

8. CVS Health website. "Message from Larry Merlo, President and CEO." February 5, 2014. https://cvshealth.com/thought-leadership/message-from-larry-merlo-president-and-ceo.

9. CVS Health website. "Message from Larry Merlo, President and

CEO." February 5, 2014. https://cvshealth.com/thought-leadership/message-from-larry-merlo-president-and-ceo.

10. LoGuirato, Brett. "Obama Releases Statement Applauding CVS on Its Decision to Stop Selling Cigarettes," *Business Insider*. February 5, 2014. https://www.businessinsider.com/obama-cvs-stopping-cigarette-sales-statement-2014-2.

11. Spera, Mark. "The 10 Marketing Secrets to Everlane's Success," GMP (Growth Marketing Pro) blog. September 21, 2018. https://www.growthmarketingpro.com/ecommerce-marketing-manual-10-secrets-everlanes-success/.

12. Ward, Sean. "All Cooped Up: How One Chick-fil-A Operator Is Redefining the Phrase," *The Chicken Wire*. February 29, 2016. https://thechickenwire.chick-fil-a.com/Inside-Chick-fil-A/All-Cooped-Up-How-One-Chick-fil-A-Operator-Is-Redefining-the-Phrase.

13. Kroger. "The Kroger Family of Companies 2018 Sustainability Report." http://sustainability.kroger.com/Kroger_CSR2018.pdf.

14. Kroger press release. "Kroger Announces Zero Hunger | Zero Waste Plan." September 19, 2017. https://www.thekrogerco.com/wp-content/uploads/2017/09/National-9-18-17-Kroger-Zero-Hunger-Zero-Waste-News-Release.pdf.

15. "The Making of the Dulux Let's Colour Project." June 29, 2010. https://www.youtube.com/watch?v=rULv_FWsfCw.

16. Johnson & Johnson website. "Nursing." https://www.discovernursing.com/sites/default/files/media/press1796178328/Campaign%20for%20Nursing%27s%20Future_Overview_5%20 3%2016.pdf.

17. Prophet website. "Be an Active Partner in Your Audiences' Passion: Lessons from Huggies." September 24, 2018.

18. IBM website. "A Culture of Think." http://www-03.ibm.com/ibm/history/ibm100/us/en/icons/think_culture/.

19. IBM website. "IBM Corporate Service Corps." https://www.ibm.com/ibm/responsibility/corporateservicecorps/#details progress.

20. Whole Foods Market website. "Local Producer Loan Program." https://www.wholefoodsmarket.com/mission-values/caring-communities/local-producer-loan-program.

21. Mackey, John and Raj Sisodia. *Conscious Capitalism* (Boston: Harvard Business Review Press, 2013) p. 131.

Chapter 6

1. Bahadur, Nina. "Dove Real Beauty Sketches Ad Becomes Most-Watched Advertisement Of All Time, Company Claims," *Huffington*

Post. May 20, 2013. https://www.huffingtonpost.com/2013/05/20/
dove-real-beauty-sketches-ad-becomes-most-watched-
advertisement-of-all-time_n_3307012.html.

2. D&AD website. "Case Study: Always #LikeAGirl." https://www.
dandad.org/en/d-ad-always-like-a-girl-campaign-case-study-
insights/.

3. Unilever press release. "Unilever's Sustainable Living Plan continues
to fuel growth." October 5, 2018. https://www.unilever.com/news/
press-releases/2018/unilevers-sustainable-living-plan-continues-to-
fuel-growth.html.

4. Buckley, Thomas and Matthew Campbell. "If Unilever Can't
Make Feel-Good Capitalism Work, Who Can?," *Bloomberg
Businessweek.* August 31, 2017. https://www.bloomberg.com/news/
features/2017-08-31/if-unilever-can-t-make-feel-good-capitalism-
work-who-can.

5. Sweeney, Erica. "Study: Brands with a purpose grow 2X faster than
others," Marketing Dive. April 19, 2018. https://www.marketingdive.
com/news/study-brands-with-a-purpose-grow-2x-faster-than-
others/521693/.

6. Faw, Larissa. "Report: Majority Of Global Consumers Are 'Belief-
Driven' Buyers," MediaPost. October 2, 2018. https://www.
mediapost.com/publications/article/325911/report-majority-of-
global-consumers-are-belief-d.html.

7. Edelman Earned Brand. "Brands Take a Stand," October 2018. https://
www.edelman.com/sites/default/files/2018-10/2018_Edelman_
Earned_Brand_Global_Report.pdf?utm_source=website&utm_
campaign=2018_edelman_earned_brand_global_report_download.

8. Hein, Bettina. "Pixability's CEO shares new cause-related marketing
research: Why brands shouldn't be afraid to take a stand,"
Think with Google. July 2017. https://www.thinkwithgoogle.com/
advertising-channels/video/cause-related-marketing-purpose-
driven-ads/.

9. Walshe, Peter. "10 traits of megabrands," *Admap.* February 2016.
http://zenithinfostation.my/wp-content/uploads/2016/05/test-1.pdf.

10. Atkin, Douglas. *The Culting of Brands* (New York: Portfolio, 2004) p. 96.

11. Bradberry, Travis. "Why the Best Leaders Have Conviction,"
Forbes. June 28, 2016. https://www.forbes.com/sites/
travisbradberry/2016/06/28/why-the-best-leaders-have-
conviction/#17b0e2fb1c8d.

12. Sinek, Simon. "How great leaders inspire action," TEDxPuget Sound.
September 2009. https://www.ted.com/talks/simon_sinek_how_great_
leaders_inspire_action.

13. "Best marketing strategy ever!" April 21, 2013. https://www.youtube.com/watch?v=keCwRdbwNQY&t=307s.

14. Anderson, Stacy. "2017 Cone Communications CSR Study: Consumers Want Brands That Share Their Values & Beliefs," We First Branding blog. https://www.wefirstbranding.com/consumers/2017-cone-communications-csr-study-consumers-want-brands-share-values-beliefs/.

15. Schaefer, Wolfgang and JP Kuehlwein. *Rethinking Prestige Branding* (London: Kogan Page, 2015) p. 15.

16. "Harley-Davidson: Live By It." September 15, 2006. https://www.youtube.com/watch?v=U2olCKnTVPI&t=11s.

17. Wikipedia website. "Harley Owners Group." https://en.wikipedia.org/wiki/Harley_Owners_Group.

18. Garfield, Bob and Doug Levy. *Can't Buy Me Like* (New York: Portfolio, 2013) p. 71.

19. Jones, Mark and Nicole Manktelow. "How Lush Has Grown Without Spending a Dime on Advertising," CMO. November 28, 2017. https://www.cmo.com/interviews/articles/2017/11/9/the-cmo-show-natasha-ritz-brand-communications-manager-lush-cosmetics.html#gs.sgbE3Hk.

20. Corporate Executive Board. "Vending on Values." December 2012.

21. Hosford, Christopher. "It Takes Courage," *B-to-B Marketer*. Winter 2016. p. 8.

22. Hiscox website. http://www.hiscox.com/small-business-insurance/blog/new-hiscox-ad-campaign-impossible/.

23. Sharp, Byron Sharp. *How Brands Grow* (Victoria, Australia: Oxford University Press, 2010).

24. Airbnb. "Airbnb Introduces the Bélo: The Story of a Symbol of Belonging." July 24, 2014. https://www.youtube.com/watch?v=nMITXMrrVQU.

25. Borgstrom, Kirsten. "Study Shows Pure Michigan Campaign Effectiveness Positive Return on Investment Generated," Press Release by the Michigan Economic Development Corporation. April 16, 2008. https://www.michigan.org/pressreleases/study-shows-pure-michigan-campaign-effectiveness-br-positive-return-on-investment-generated.

26. WARC. "adidas Originals: Original is Never Finished." 2018. https://www.warc.com/content/article/adidas_Originals_Original_is_Never_Finished/122315.

27. Pallotta, Frank. "New York Times touts subscriber growth with a jab at Trump," CNN Business. February 2, 2017. https://money.cnn.com/2017/02/02/media/new-york-times-subscribers-trump/index.html.

Chapter 7

1. Diamond, Dan. "The ALS Ice Bucket Challenge Has Raised $100 Million — And Counting," *Forbes*. August 29, 2014. https://www.forbes.com/sites/dandiamond/2014/08/29/the-als-ice-bucket-challenge-has-raised-100m-but-its-finally-cooling-off/#5918ffa75cfb.

2. Lindstrom, Martin. "Opinionated Branding Proves Powerful," Brand Strategy Insider blog. November 17, 2008. https://www.brandingstrategyinsider.com/2008/11/opinionated-branding-proves-powerful.html#.W71Wry2ZOu4.

3. Edelman Earned Brand. "Brands Take a Stand," October 2018. https://www.edelman.com/sites/default/files/2018-10/2018_Edelman_Earned_Brand_Global_Report.pdf?utm_source=website&utm_campaign=2018_edelman_earned_brand_global_report_download.

4. Hein, Bettina. "Pixability's CEO shares new cause-related marketing research: Why brands shouldn't be afraid to take a stand," Think with Google. July 2017. https://www.thinkwithgoogle.com/advertising-channels/video/cause-related-marketing-purpose-driven-ads/.

5. Precourt, Geoffrey. "Pulling the curtain back on the 'terrifying' Fearless Girl," WARC. March 2018. https://www.warc.com/content/article/event-reports/pulling_the_creative_curtain_back_on_the_terrifying_fearless_girl/121627.

6. Mullen, Jethro. "Johnnie Walker is being replaced by Jane (on some bottles)," *CNN Business*. February 27, 2018. http://money.cnn.com/2018/02/27/news/companies/johnnie-walker-women-jane-walker/index.html.

7. Shelton Group. "Brands & Stands: Social Purpose is the New Black." 2018. https://sheltongrp.com/insights/brands-stands-social-purpose-is-the-new-black.

8. Allen-Mersh, Will, Emma Batho and Ayesha Walawalkar. "The radicalisation of Persil: How prisoners helped us restore conviction in the brand," WARC. 2017. https://www.warc.com/content/article/apg/the_radicalisation_of_persil_how_prisoners_helped_us_restore_conviction_in_the_brand/112593.

9. American Express website. "Shop Small." https://www.americanexpress.com/us/small-business/shop-small/about?linknav=us-open-shopsmall-home-nationallanding-sbshistory.

10. Izzo, John and Jeff Vanderwielen. *The Purpose Revolution* (Oakland, California: Berrett-Koehler Publishers, 2018) p. 24.

11. Nudd, Tim. "REI Will Be Closed on Black Friday, and Pay Its 12,000 Employees Not to Work That Day," *Adweek.* October 27, 2015. https://www.adweek.com/creativity/rei-will-be-closed-black-friday-and-pay-its-12000-employees-not-work-day-167780/.

12. REI Co-op website. "Newsroom." http://newsroom.rei.com/news/corporate/a-life-outdoors-is-life-well-lived.htm.

13. Parkhurst, Emily. "That REI Black Friday stunt? It worked. REI posts largest-ever membership growth," *Puget Sound Business Journal.* March 15, 2016. https://www.bizjournals.com/seattle/news/2016/03/15/that-rei-black-friday-stunt-it-worked-rei-posts.html.

14. Pasquarelli, Adrianne. "How CVS Won by Not Selling Cigarettes," *AdAge.* October 20, 2016. https://adage.com/article/special-report-ana-annual-meeting-2016/cvs-won-selling-cigarettes/306384/.

15. Rupp, Lindsey. "Patagonia's Stand Against Public-Land Cuts Overwhelms Website," *Bloomberg.* December 5, 2017. https://www.bloomberg.com/news/articles/2017-12-05/patagonia-s-stand-against-public-land-cuts-overwhelms-website.

16. Oster, Erik. "Majority of Consumers Want Brands to Take a Stand on Social and Political Issues, According to New Study," *Adweek.* January 12, 2018. https://www.adweek.com/brand-marketing/majority-of-consumers-want-brands-to-take-a-stand-on-social-and-political-issues-according-to-new-study/.

17. Kirkpatrick, David. "4A's: 58% of consumers dislike brands getting political," *Marketing Dive.* May 25, 2017. https://www.marketingdive.com/news/4as-58-of-consumers-dislike-brands-getting-political/443538/.

Conclusion

1. Kristol, William. "A Deep Devotion to the Cause of Human Liberty," *The Weekly Standard.* August 26, 2018. https://www.weeklystandard.com/william-kristol/john-mccain-1936-2018.

Index

About the Author

 **Matt Carcieri** is one of the world's foremost "purposologists," having worked on purpose with more than a hundred companies and brands.

He began his career as a marketing executive at Procter & Gamble, where, for fifteen years, he pioneered purpose-driven brand building inside the world's largest advertiser. As an in-house expert on the topic, he spearheaded purpose work on most of P&G's billion-dollar brands.

Today, he is an independent consultant and an affiliate of The Jim Stengel Group, a think tank and consulting practice founded by the former CMO of P&G. In those roles, Matt has helped to define and activate purpose for companies across a variety of industries – from financial services and insurance to health care and hospitality.

Matt holds an M.B.A. from Georgetown University and has co-authored works in three marketing compilations, including *Kellogg on Branding* (Wiley, 2019). He is a sought-after speaker on both the business and college circuits.

He lives in Cincinnati, Ohio with his wife and three sons.